S.O.S.
Alternatives
to Capitalism

RICHARD SWIFT

About the author
Richard Swift is a journalist/activist who works in print and radio. He was for more than two decades an editor of the New Internationalist magazine. He has written a number of books on themes as diverse as mosquitoes and street gangs. His current interests include forms of radical democracy and ecological degrowth alternatives. He lives in Montreal, Quebec.

Acknowledgements
To my editor Chris Brazier who makes the words that merely walk start to run. To my comrades in Montreal and Toronto and so many other places. To those close to me who continue to put up with me. And to the sages who are no longer with us, particularly André Gorz, EP Thompson, Daniel Singer and Kurt Vonnegut.

S.O.S.
Alternatives
to Capitalism

RICHARD SWIFT

S.O.S.: Alternatives to Capitalism
First published in 2014 by
New Internationalist Publications Ltd
55 Rectory Road
Oxford OX4 1BW, UK
newint.org

Cover design: Andrew Kokotka
Design: Juha Sorsa
Imprint editor: Chris Brazier

Printed by T J International Limited, Cornwall, UK
who hold environmental accreditation ISO 14001.

British Library Cataloguing-in-Publication Data
A catalogue record for this book is available from the British
Library.

Library of Congress Cataloging-in-Publication Data
A catalog record for this book is available
from the Library of Congress.

ISBN: 978-1-78026-170-6

Contents

Foreword

'What is not possible, however, is to even think about transforming the world without a utopia, without a project.'

Paulo Freire

In these times the search for alternatives to capitalism is imperative. The world's economy is in total disarray, having emerged from a very deep recession only to suffer what appears to be a prolonged stagnation in which governments cannot determine which is most perilous: spiraling public debt, looming deflation or dangerous new asset bubbles. Public policies lurch wildly to counter one, then the other of these alleged threats, while ignoring the fast disappearance of stable employment that pays a living wage and its replacement by precarious employment, or no employment at all. The rush to cut back public services and pensions and attack unions in desperate waves of austerity only exacerbates the underlying economic crisis.

And there is a still more urgent environmental crisis facing us. As Naomi Klein recently declared at the founding convention of Canada's largest private sector union, Unifor: 'Our current economic model is not only waging war on workers, on communities, on public services and social safety nets. It's waging war on the life-support systems of the planet itself – the conditions for life on earth.' In his exploration of alternatives to capitalism, Richard Swift sees no solution in state socialism, whether of the communist or social democratic variety, as both impose socialism from above. Echoing a view first expounded by the late Robert Heilbroner, he argues that 'state communism was not really an alternative to capitalism at all but merely a transitional form of it which allowed certain large "backward" societies hitherto blocked in their developmental path, to move towards their own peculiar model of autocratic capitalism'. As for the social democratic variety, it long ago abandoned any hope of replacing capitalism in favor of the attempt to moderate its most predatory aspects. Only very occasionally, as in the case of Allende's Chile in the early 1970s, has capitalism found it necessary to engage in military exercises to destroy elected social democratic governments since, as Swift notes, the 'tame Center-Left proved sufficiently accommodating to the needs of capital'.

As examples of evolving real-world alternatives to capitalism Swift applauds elements of Venezuela's Bolivarian Revolution initiated by the late Hugo Chávez, in particular the vast expansion of co-operative enterprises and the devolving of power to local community councils; he also casts an approving eye on Brazil's experience with participatory budgeting in Porto Alegre and elsewhere. At the same time, he warns of the tensions in Venezuela and other manifestations of Latin America's '21st-century socialism', pointing out the contradictions between reforms from below and the bureaucratic machinery that breeds personal corruption and impedes democratic initiatives.

One of the finest chapters of *SOS: Alternatives to Capitalism* is devoted to tracing the legacy of anarchism from Proudhon and Bakunin through the Sixties New Left and its notion of participatory democracy to the anti-globalization, autonomous and Occupy movements. As Swift points out, there is a perennial tension within anarchism. On the one side are those who advocate the forcible overthrow of power through acts of mass defiance. On the other are those who promote building spaces and practices of self-rule within the fissures of the capitalist system so as to challenge state structures by example. The latter strand includes worker-owned producer co-operatives, housing co-operatives and credit unions. He argues persuasively that, however noble these efforts may be, and however satisfying to those who participate in them, 'if there is no decisive challenge to the logic of capitalism, such alternatives will continue to be marginalized and deformed'. Swift also strongly opposes both anarchist rejection of the state in any form and Leninist fantasies of smashing the state: 'the days of storming the Bastille and the Winter Palace are things of the past,' he concludes. Against these two dead ends he adduces a third position: responding to popular needs and extending the notion of democracy to embed it in communities and workplaces.

In his survey of alternatives, Swift is most sympathetic to the current of thought taking shape under the rubric of 'ecosocialism'. What differentiates ecosocialism from the socialism that preceded it is its rejection of a set of assumptions shared with capitalism itself: the necessity of economic growth, and the corresponding license to exploit the supposedly endless bounty of the natural world coupled with an uncritical belief in the beneficence of technology. Against some impressive efforts by scholars like John Bellamy Foster and others to paint a picture of Marx as an ecological philosopher *avant la lettre*, Swift correctly notes that while Marx explored a 'metabolic rift' that capitalism had opened up between humans and nature, this was a sidebar at best, coexisting with 'a celebration of material progress as the path to human advancement'.

Swift is emphatically dismissive of Green parties that first emerged in the 1980s: like social democratic parties before them, they soon gave up any notion of replacing capitalism even though, as he says, it is 'pretty obvious that both inequality and growth are built into the very DNA of the capitalist system. Capitalism can never be about selling us less, living in a more modest way or reducing inequalities.' Having avoided presenting themselves as any kind of overall ecological alternative to capitalism, they are left with promoting such nebulous goals as 'green growth', 'green jobs' and market-based solutions such as the carbon tax.

SOS: Alternatives to Capitalism deservedly devotes ample space to the concept of degrowth. A degrowth economy would feature reduced working hours, a much expanded public sector, a guaranteed annual income, allocating resources democratically so that shortages are distributed fairly. It would also, to the extent that it is possible, prioritize the local in everything: energy and agricultural systems, the disposal/reuse/recycling of waste and so on. How could we ensure that wealth would be redirected away from paper speculation and harmful production and towards alternative projects of sustainability that would support democratic degrowth? For Swift, socializing the financial services industry, including converting the banks into public utilities, would be a good place to start. A degrowth economy would have to be a planned economy and Swift is to be commended for acknowledging that fact, despite not having sufficient space to tackle it thoroughly.

In his search for a way forward, it is important to Swift to say that: 'The post-growth alternative to capitalism needs to be different in its very language. It must move beyond earlier preoccupations with class struggle, while maintaining its commitments to equality and democracy.' While in general terms this sentiment may be widely shared among readers of this book, the assertion that class struggle in particular no longer has a place in movements of post-capitalism will obviously be controversial, including among many who share his ecosocialist philosophy.

With *SOS: Alternatives to Capitalism*, Swift joins a growing strand of 21st-century literature that explores radically different ways of organizing our economy and politics. These include, among others, Robin Hahnel's *Of the People, For the People*; Joel Kovel's *The Enemy of Nature*; Michael Lebowitz's *The Socialist Alternative*; and Erik Olin Wright's *Envisioning Real Utopias*.

In my view Swift is commendably judicious in how he sorts through the contested turf of left thinking, but in so thoroughly and decisively dismissing so much of what passes for left politics – visions, strategies and all – this book is bound to generate much heated discussion.

It can't begin too soon for, as the US anthropologist David Graeber has written, without the Swifts of this world, 'we are left in the bizarre situation of watching the capitalist system crumbling before our very eyes, at just the moment everyone had finally concluded no other system would be possible'.

Cy Gonick
Cy Gonick is a senior statesman of the Canadian Left. He is both an activist and author as well as professor emeritus in the economics department at the University of Manitoba. He is the founder and long-time editor of *Canadian Dimension* magazine.

Introduction: A sad and beautiful world in peril

It is pretty obvious that our world is in trouble. Well, maybe not the earth itself or even the global ecosystem that calls it home. These are likely to survive in one form or another so long as their star (the sun) doesn't burn out. It is more the place occupied by the human species that is in question as we destroy the ecological conditions necessary to support us in the numbers and style to which we have grown accustomed. That's right – we are doing it to ourselves. Species suicide.

'Oh, here we go,' you might say, 'another one of those "end-of-the-world-is-nigh" books.' Well, it's true nonetheless. We are doing it incrementally, by stealth, like one of those new bombers you can't detect until it's too late, or like the drones that blow you up when you think you are safe hanging out with your family on the rooftop. We think we are OK but the evidence is mounting that we are not: increasing instances of often deadly extreme weather; stultifying urban environments like those of Beijing and myriad other Chinese cities that are choking on coal smoke; our sad dependence on the oil economy with its toxic spills; explosions of all kinds as we heat the climate to cooking point. Renewable resources – fresh water, fertile soil, global fish stocks – are fast being rendered non-renewable by greed and wasteful misuse. Then there is the human cost in lives of precarious labor, huge refugee populations and fully one in six of humans barely able to survive on pennies a day. I could, of course, go on but I don't want to discourage you at this early stage.

That's the sad part – so what about the beautiful? The list is almost endless. A Canadian lake during a misty dawn; a walk in the fields of the English west country; the sounds of a jungle at night; dolphins playing in the waves; the bounty of colorful fish that inhabits any coral reef – and that's just the natural world. Then there's the idiosyncratic human species – from your children embarking on their wonderstruck discovery of life in all its diversity and glory right through to that odd fellow in Montreal who dresses up in a panda suit to protect student demonstrators from police violence. When our best natures aren't suppressed, we can be loving, funny, carefree, courageous, thoughtful and capable of wondrous acts of generosity.

Of course, we won't always be this way. Sometimes we will be small-minded and mean, narcissistic and self-serving – downright nasty. We will always have these competing traits. So what we need to do is to organize the world in such a way as to encourage our better selves and discourage our narrow-minded and nasty side. Our current system of capital accumulation (known as corporate capitalism) does just the opposite. This champions and fosters narrow-minded self-interest and greed as the cornerstone of all that is human. It also fosters inequality and powerlessness on a massive scale and is driving us in the direction of eco-destruction – including of the aforementioned lakes, reefs, jungles and dolphins.

It has reached the point where the Marxist theorist Frederick Jameson can say without irony that it is easier to think of the end of the world than the end of capitalism. For, while the world is doing badly, capitalism is getting along just fine. Oh sure, there are economic crises and financial blow-ups, but the goods are still being delivered to those at the top of the pile with an enviably smooth efficiency and the general public still seem to accept the corporate message that 'there is no alternative'. This is, of course, a self-serving lie.

The purpose of this book is to tease out what such genuine alternatives to capitalism might look like. It looks at what the past experience of such alternatives has been, at the issues and problems that have haunted them – the paths not taken. This is a bittersweet history of rich diversity marked by massacre, noble failure and tepid success. The book then moves into the present to seek a way out of the maze of life-threatening inequality and eco-catastrophe.

The history of capitalism is, of course, tied up with the various waves of the industrial revolution, with its attendant technological advances – steam, carbon, nuclear and now cyber, to pick an arbitrary few. Today, some advocates of alternatives to capitalism hold that industrialism itself, which was so shaped by the needs of capitalists for profit and control, needs to be thrown off; their view is that human society needs to return to a kind of neo-primitivist sensibility, abandoning our technological fixes and consumer addictions. Others, who are no less opposed to the inequalities of wealth and power that scar capitalism, take the contrary position on questions of modernity. For orthodox Marxists and many of their antecedents, for many liberal reformers, for those committed to the 'development' of the Global South, the problem with capitalism is that it is shackling modernity rather than abetting it. This is a vital point (though far from the only one) that divides critics who think about what an alternative to capitalism might look like.

The conceit of progress that is built into modern-day capitalism produces a number of common myths. The first is the widespread belief that we are better off now than we have ever been. The second is that we have no alternative but to continue in the direction of corporate growth or dire consequences will ensue. The third is that there is a kind of trans-historical human nature that condemns us all to act only in our own narrow self-interest. The fourth is that our present state was fashioned more or less democratically, with dissent only from the backward and foolish. The fifth is that we need constant speed-up in production and work and society as a whole in order to ensure we can meet our (often unsustainable) needs. The sixth is that science and technology alone can save us from whatever problems corporate growth produces. And the seventh one, which perhaps underpins the others, is that all we have to do is make sure the pie keeps growing.

Taken together, these make up a powerful arsenal of *status quo* 'common sense' weapons that need to be unpicked so as to expose their profoundly unhistorical and dead-end nature. This volume will try to do just that, as it explores alternative ways of living and loving life.

1

Sources of hope – life before capitalism

Many values that today's societies take for granted are very recent interlopers in human history. Life before capitalism was not devoid of pleasure – and was certainly not as individualistic. Modern attempts to create alternatives can draw inspiration from the past, not only from less acquisitive, more communitarian societies, but also from heroic examples of resistance.

'If you want to find out more, you have to move backward against the flow of time, while simultaneously moving forward.'
Cees Nooteboom[1]

Capitalism as a total world system is a relatively new part of human experience. It has its roots in the 16th and 17th centuries, which means that it has been around for four or five hundred years at most, while we humans (*Homo sapiens*) have been around for 200,000 years, reaching anatomical maturity some 50,000 years ago. Our ancestors (the less predatory *Homo erectus*) go back over a million years. By these measures capitalism is merely the blink of an eye.

Yet for most people living today this short time span is difficult to grasp. Partly this is because we have no relatives that remember pre-capitalism, and the oral tradition that used to pass historical knowledge from generation to generation has largely been disrupted by first literate and then media culture. There have been so many rapid technological changes over the past century that they add up to a kind of rupture in human memory. We have become future-oriented, addicted to novelty and 'into' discovering (and possessing) the latest thing in our rootless consumer universe. Pre-capitalism is today the preserve of academic specialists or isolated tribal remnants and remote villages. Yet it is well worth reflecting on what life was like before capitalism.

Happiness is not a modern invention

The doctrine of progress that accompanied the rise of capitalism would have it that, in the words of that early advocate of the rule of property, Thomas Hobbes, life before capitalism was 'nasty, brutish and short'.[2] This is a self-serving half-truth. There was certainly brutality and slavery, and the absolute power of warlords and despots was only partially kept in check by custom and the limited killing capacity of the primitive weaponry then to hand. Human happiness, reflection, resilience and initiative are not, however, creations of market society but flourished in medieval abbeys, amongst Paleolithic hunter gatherers, in Neolithic villages, ancient Greek city-states, among the pastoralists whose herds wandered Asia and Africa, in the indigenous communities of the Americas. In all periods of history from the Paleolithic through the Neolithic right up to the Late Feudal, people enjoyed their food, loved their children, thought about the universe and its meaning and tried to live according to their values.

The further you go back, the more disdainful the judgments of the modern conceits of progress come to seem. The notion that the lives of early hunter-gatherers were impossibly difficult is today challenged by many anthropologists, including Marshall Sahlins in his classic work *Stone Age Economics*.[3] Sahlins makes the case that hunter-gatherers had far more leisure time than we do today (provided, of course, that we are lucky enough to have jobs). Their lives depended on seasonal factors and the bounty of the local ecosystem. It is now widely accepted that traditional hunter-gatherer societies often took the form of a kind of primitive communism, which was horizontal in its organizational structure. The North American tribes of the Iroquois Confederacy or the Pueblos of the US Southwest, who lived in communal decentralized communities, were more the rule, while the imperial Aztecs of Mexico and hierarchical Incas of Peru were more the exception. These horizontal communities show a rich variation in organization, with women often playing an important role in government, as they did among the Iroquois. The French anthropologist Pierre Clastres argues that political arrangements in many tribal societies were put in place precisely as insurance against the emergence of despotic power (in other words, 'the state').[4] He held that such arrangements only broke down with the emergence of a caste of priestly leaders who claimed a special relationship with a higher deity. The move away from hunter-gatherer societies to agricultural communities and eventually large-scale hydrological agriculture (which took place initially in riverine societies in what is today Iraq and Egypt) also saw the advent of a much stricter division of labor and the rise of the coercive political power of the state. Life expectancy actually fell in this new situation.

The kind of individualism that has developed under capitalism was virtually unknown in early societies and would have appeared strange indeed to both hunter-gatherers and the first agriculturalists. Right up until the decline of classic feudalism and the emergence of the city-states of Italy and Holland, followed by mercantilist England, what we think of as self-serving human nature was the exception in a world hemmed in by social and religious obligation. The rise of the system of Atlantic trade, including colonialism and the globalization of slavery, meant a wholesale assault on these traditional systems of organization – rich in their variety from imperial China, to Aztec Mexico and the Ashanti kingdoms of West Africa. Traditional systems varied from large-scale centralized empires to localized (and jealously defended) traditions of self-rule. The Aymara and Quechua peoples of the Andean highlands are today using the pre-Inca tradition of *ayllu* (a self-governing, highly flexible form of home community based on collective rights) as a way of resisting outside domination. For these people (and many others), these traditions are not museum pieces but can be 're-inscribed' as part of a living tradition that has shown a remarkable ability to adapt in order to survive.

Losing our diversity

The point is not that these were the pre-capitalist 'good old days' but that, until relatively recently, life was different from that which we experience in today's market and commodity-dominated society. Sometimes it was better; sometimes worse. But it was always different. This is a truth that the partisans of contemporary market progress like to avoid; perhaps because what was different before could be different again. It is the diversity of real possibility that we are losing under the homogenizing influence of corporate capitalism. Today, the large institutions that shape the world economy (the International Monetary Fund and the World Trade Organization) lay down rules of trade and investment that they insist that we all must live by from Mongolia to Mozambique. They bury centuries-old differences in an avalanche of commercial rules so as to bring order in the form of their particular notion of profit-based calculation. These rules are usually shaped not to accord with the desires and needs of the people most affected but rather to provide a degree of predictability for the large corporate organizations and capital or bond markets that structure finance. Their greatest horror is when some significant player steps outside their rules by threatening default on debt, violating investor 'rights' or making wealthy creditors (rather than ordinary citizens) take the economic cold plunge. Such heresies can be remarkably successful ways of dealing with economic crisis, as populist governments in Argentina (2002) and Iceland (2008) have recently proved.

Anthropology teaches us that diversity in rules, habits and social forms has always been the human way. This is why it would be easy to fill these pages with examples of those who have insisted (and still insist) on resisting capitalist monoculture, whether that comes in the form of self-serving commercial rules, politics as the sole preserve of professional politicians or the culture of celebrity and gadget worship. But too often the insistence on difference becomes just another niche marketing opportunity. The system feeds on the very dissatisfaction and predictability it has manufactured to sell new forms of 'renegade authenticity', particularly to young people desperate to escape the boredom and limits they have inherited. Thus revolt easily becomes just another species of the rootless consumer appetite that drives us on. What we need is to take strength from the spirit of our many ancestors and look for real diversity – not as a consumer choice but as an insistence on living and valuing differently.

Particular societies bring out a variety of different potentials in human beings, encouraging some while discouraging others. Some of these point in a quite different direction from that of our current market society. The Reformation and its followers in Germany and elsewhere worked to build a communalist New Jerusalem. The Potlatch ceremony indicated a very different attitude towards wealth, in which the most successful of tribal chiefs on the North American west coast displayed their wealth by giving it away; accumulation for its own sake would have been considered an anathema. Feudal reciprocity was the way in which the titled aristocracy took some responsibility for the well-being of their vassals. Harvest festivals were the way in which agricultural societies paid homage to natural bounty for sustaining them.

The commons played a large role in both economy and society all through the experience of pre-capitalist societies of various types – the commons being a shared resource from which each had the right to draw their livelihood, even if this livelihood was unequally shared under feudal conditions. The health of the commons – pasture land, gardens, woodland, water supply – was the concern of all. Economy was, as Karl Polanyi has so brilliantly analyzed, 'socially embedded' in such societies and subject to the prevailing values of that particular society rather than the kind of all-determining external force it has become under capitalism.[5] As market relations began to disentangle the economic from the social and cultural, fewer and fewer human checks remained to slow down or redirect the disembodied drive for profit. Today we experience the economy as a kind of out-of-control external force disconnected from human will. We speak of the stock market, for example, as if it is a living person – sometimes confident, sometimes jittery, feeling robust, suffering an attack of nerves and so on; a kind of Old Testament Mammon god.

On the other hand, it is undeniable that the rise of market society kicked off what was to become a dramatic growth in individual rights. While many of these rights had to do with property, others formed the basis of the current constitutional order, of what we think of as democratic governance (at least in certain times in certain societies). Ironically, such rights continue to be used to oppose the concentration of wealth and power that was also a by-product of the rise of market society – which explains the very ambivalent feelings about these freedoms displayed by theorists and partisans of corporate society.[6]

The shift to capitalist ways of doing things (the concentration of private property, wage labor, turning environmental resources into disposable commodities) came with sharp resistance from many quarters. Historians such as EP Thompson, whose brilliant *The Making of the English Working Class* charted the early defense of the democratic commons in England,[7] have documented how people across Europe were dragged kicking and screaming into the factories and poorhouses of early capitalism. Where capitalism in its colonial cloak ran up against the indigenous societies of the Americas or the more structured states of Asia, the response was every bit as fierce. The 'Indians' of the Americas proved not only unwilling to give up their way of life and territory but those who survived the colonial onslaught made for a very poor agricultural and industrial workforce. This is where the famous capitalist 'initiative' to create the triangular slave trade between Africa, Europe and the plantation economies of the Americas came into play. African workers, torn from their societies, proved a more efficient (if hardly willing) solution to the labor shortage. The slave revolt in Haiti, and its inspirational influence on the African diaspora in the Americas, illustrates the fierce resistance to a life of hard labor in the service of profit.

Communitarian alternatives

The ability of capitalism to recreate itself through destabilizing crises and the uprooting of peoples keeps this sense of discontent forever brewing. Today, many of the ideas about alternatives to capitalism are rooted in pre-capitalist communitarian traditions. One such can be seen in the work of the indigenous Bolivian sociologist Félix Patzi Paco, who champions the tradition of *ayllu* alluded to above. His is not some narrow backwoods project or anthropological oddity, but rather:

> '*an invitation to organize and re-inscribe communal systems all over the world – systems that have been erased and dismantled by the increasing expansion of the capitalist economy, which the European left has been unable to halt. If ayllus and markas are*

> *the singular memory and organization of communities in the Andes, then it is the other memories of communal organization around the globe which predate and survived the advent of capitalism which make possible the idea of a communal system today – one not mapped out in advance by any ideology, or any simple return to the past. The Zapatista dictum of the need for "a world in which many worlds fit" springs to mind as we try to imagine a planet of communal systems in a pluri-versal, not uni-versal, world order.*[8]

Not only did burgeoning capitalism meet with fierce resistance but this dissatisfaction has led to a constant parade of ideas and projects to create an alternative. Some, such as socialism and anarchism, have been persistent poles of opposition, while others have taken the form of smaller practical and utopian projects. The modern era, dating back to, say, the times of the French and US revolutions, has seen thousands of such communitarian alternatives come and go. Some have been religious in their inspiration (the Anabaptists and Hutterites, or later the Russian Doukhobors, for example) while others have tended towards the secular. Some were more vertical in their organization, often gathered around a charismatic figure who welded absolute authority over the community. Others were more horizontal, being fiercely democratic. Most aspired to some egalitarian ideal that was a reaction to the polarization of wealth and power that has been an abiding feature of capitalism, including the communities created by Winstanley and the Diggers (the radical wing of the English Revolution), or, later, New Harmony in Pennsylvania or the Oneida Community in upstate New York inspired by John Noyes.[9] Such attempts to escape the rule of the capitalist market can be seen right through to the 1960s back-to-the-land movement and the sustainable eco-communities that still exist across Europe and the Americas.

Today, alternatives to capitalism continue to survive and thrive in a number of living forms and social movements. The emphasis shifts with the context. Now there is a new language underpinning new ideas – as when the prefix 'eco' is added to that old warhorse 'socialism'. Ecosocialism contains a suspicion of technology and the gospel of progress that was unfamiliar back in the days of state-socialist Five Year Plans or various social-democratic schemes of modernization. There are new movements that advocate doing things slowly – slow food, slow cities, even slow money. Some speak of radical autonomy, in response to a state increasingly divorced from its democratic pretensions. Others aim to rethink the entire enterprise of economic growth and speak of a future based on degrowth. There is also now an attempt to fuse the struggles against poverty and wealth into a common notion of a democratic sufficiency in which all might share. Today's advocates of an alternative to wasteful capitalism have their roots in past human experiences. They can all find voices of past dissent that still speak to them and offer possibilities of roads not yet taken.

1 Cees Nooteboom, *All Soul's Day*, Harcourt Books, New York, 1997. **2** Thomas Hobbes, *Leviathan*, Penguin Classic, 1981. **3** Marshall Sahlins, *Stone Age Economics*, Routledge, New York, 1989. **4** Pierre Clastres, *Society against the State*, Zone Books, Cambridge, 1990. **5** Karl Polanyi, *The Great Transformation*, Beacon Press, Boston, 1944. **6** Samuel Bowles and Herb Gintis, *Democracy and Capitalism*, Basic Books, New York, 1986. **7** EP Thompson, *The Making of the English Working Class*, Vintage, New York, 1966. **8** Walter Mignolo, 'The Communal and the Decolonial' *Turbulence (Ideas for Movement)*, nin.tl/1a9hwZY **9** Kenneth Rexroth, *Communalism: from its origins to the 20th century*, Seabury Press, New York, 1974.

2

Capitalism: a system of reckless resilience

How capitalism developed – and why it depends upon 'creative destruction'. The rise of neoliberalism as a political philosophy and the transformation of old enemies such as Russia and China into authoritarian free marketeers. And why capitalism is beyond the control even of the captains of finance.

'The most convincing and enduring foe of the global financial economy ultimately is the global financial economy itself.'
Ulrich Beck[1]

What is the problem with capitalism anyway? Hasn't it delivered modernity and prosperity over the centuries? Has a better economic system ever emerged, offering a more efficient way for allocating resources? Isn't the invisible hand of the market the only way for billions of people to interact economically without falling under stultifying bureaucratic control?

Those who make the case for capitalism vary from its most sophisticated economic thinkers (such as Adam Smith, Friedrich Hayek and Milton Friedman) to the thousands of graduates of business schools who all sing from the same songbook of market perfection. Even the best-known liberal critics of capitalism such as John Maynard Keynes and John Kenneth Galbraith saw no real alternative to it as the most efficient form of economic organization, although they were committed to finding ways to iron out its instabilities and disequilibria through the intervention of the public power of the state. But such reforms have fallen out of fashion given the ascendancy of neoliberal orthodoxy since the 1980s. Today, government after government still suffers from frozen policy imaginations in the face of the speculative bubbles that destabilize everything from public finance to the plans and dreams of ordinary people. The panicked *ad hoc* bail-out of banks and corporations 'too big to fail' and the imposition of austerity packages on the masses to pay for it now appear to be the only recipes in the public policy cookbook. By and large, government policies, despite bold words about re-establishing a coherent regime of regulation, have failed to gain much more leverage over these corporate actors than did the previous regime of speculative 'market freedom'. It was this neoliberal dispensation, obsessed with removing the regulatory shackles on the 'free' movement of capital, that allowed the creation and sale of an avalanche of unstable paper assets – secondary mortgage markets, derivatives, credit default swaps, and so on. According to the economic historian Jeff Madrick, most of these difficulties remain to be addressed:

> 'These included the lack of transparency in the derivatives markets, where prices were set in obscurity on trillions of dollars of transactions. Market theory calls for clear and open pricing information. It includes the conflicts of interest of the credit ratings agencies, which were paid by the issuers seeking high ratings. This is bound to lead to market failure. There are also the absurd compensation practices of Wall Street, which largely protected the traders and other decision-makers from the longer-term risks the stockholders were taking.'[2]

Even in the face of the obvious failures of the current phase of finance-dominated capitalism, the political class seems to have no ability (or even willingness) to regulate the destructive behavior of those wielding economic power – let alone the imagination to conceive of an alternative to capitalism. Reform of regulatory agencies such as the US Federal Reserve or the Bank of Settlements in Switzerland has largely left them toothless or subject to bad conflicts of interest. The market conditions that allowed the collapse of 2008 to occur remain a Sword of Damocles hanging over the global economy.

Historical roots

There was a time when capitalism was seen as simply one of a number of competing philosophies of political economy. It grew up in opposition to the traditionalist conservatism of big feudal landowners. It was associated from its inception with a politics that embraced the negative freedoms of non-interference with individual enterprise and conscience. Its proponents were quite skeptical of the more positive freedoms associated with a wider democracy. They feared (not without reason) that a broader majoritarian self-rule would endanger the rights to the enjoyment of property of those who by 'dint of their own efforts' had been successful in obtaining it. For theorists such as John Locke, who influenced the English Revolution, or many of the Founding Fathers who shaped the limits of the American Revolution, there was a profound distrust of mob rule. By this they meant that those without property (and perhaps even slaves) might come together to assert their interests and rights. The vision of the most radical of these theorists of the revolutions that cleared the way for capitalism to flourish was that of 'a republic of smallholders'. Men like Thomas Jefferson of Virginia or Jean-Jacques Rousseau in France might well have been horrified by the way in which today's one-per-cent corporate super-rich and their acolytes dominate economic and political decision-making. Their vision was a distinctly rural one of a sturdy and independent yeomanry and craftspeople that would form the backbone of a healthy society. Nonetheless, their emphasis on market freedom and the unrestricted right to accumulate property and riches helped to pave the way for the current pre-eminence of wealth and power. The smallholder (although still around) proved far too vulnerable to the market forces that concentrated resources in the hands of a few. A very few smallholders became successful entrepreneurs while the great majority were forced into a precarious position at the edge of the capitalist economy.

There were, of course, those who railed against the limitations of the capitalist revolutions of the 17th and 18th centuries with their narrow notions of freedom. Most famous, perhaps, were the Levellers during the English Civil War, who foresaw the inequalities of wealth and power that were to plague capitalism throughout the coming centuries. They were given short shrift by Oliver Cromwell, who first argued with and then executed them. In the 13 colonies, Thomas Paine found the American Revolution lacking in democratic substance. The radical priest Jacques Roux and his *Enragés* championed the economic rights of the poor during the French Revolution, demanding an end to private property and a classless society. Roux so alarmed Robespierre and the Jacobins that they brought trumped-up charges against him and caused him to commit suicide in his jail cell in 1794. There has always been a sense among its critics that capitalism has never really delivered on its promise of a thorough-going political democracy, a persistent sense that inequality and the rule of property consistently work to undermine the self-rule of the majority.

One of the features of capitalism that has enabled it to survive is its ability both to create and to take advantage of economic crises. This phenomenon was investigated and systematized by the political economist Joseph Schumpeter, who referred to it as a tendency for 'creative destruction'. Schumpeter saw this underlying attribute as a kind of positive resilience that keeps capitalism from collapsing under the weight of its own contradictions. For centuries, its opponents have looked to such crises as a source of hope, believing that the beast had finally overstepped the mark and could be brought to ground. These booms and busts are not new but have supplied the rhythm of the deployment of capital from the 16th century onwards, destabilizing people's lives through the enclosure of the commons, the expansion of empires, and the shift of industry from less profitable to more profitable regions. This destabilizing effect has always been a major source of the dissatisfaction with capitalism. It has inspired people to search for alternatives that provide a more balanced and stable form of existence, where they can count on regular access to the fundamentals of their survival – food and shelter, peace and community. Capitalism constantly puts these things at risk in its restless search for new avenues of profitable growth. Oddly, this has aroused dissatisfaction from both conservative and radical sources: conservative, in the sense that people struggle to preserve whatever well-being they have managed to achieve but find it constantly threatened; radical, in the sense that the search for security calls forth the need to imagine and fight for a new order of things in which people control capital rather than the other way around.

Those who, for moral, economic or political reasons, are opposed to the insecurity, inequality and egoism that seem inevitable consequences of the capitalist way of operating do, however, face a significant uphill challenge. Not only has capitalism shown great resilience in overcoming the periodic crises it has faced but it has also even been embraced by its one-time ideological opponents: state socialism in China and the countries of the former Soviet bloc. These societies have now embraced the market as the most effective economic driver of future development. Today, most of the public economies of such countries have come under the sway of private capital – much of it foreign. China, in particular, has become 'the workshop of the world', with its labor force working under extremely exploitative conditions within a political system that still proclaims itself communist. Here, opportunities for resistance by workers are much more limited than they were in the early days of industrialization in the Western world. With few exceptions, trade unions are imposed from above and work with management to help discipline the workforce. Any worker resistance is met with staunch measures by police or private security forces. While some local worker complaints are allowed if sent through official channels, overall co-ordination of worker resistance, direct action or critiques of 'communist' capitalism that joins up all the analytic dots are all vigorously suppressed. Yet these dissenting activities still go on. 'Mass incidents' of labor unrest in China rose from 70,000 in 2004 to 180,000 in 2010 with virtually every economic sector affected.[3] This has led some to identify contemporary China as 'the epicenter of global labor unrest'.[4] It is certainly one of the ironies of the modern world that what remains of this failed experiment in communism is being used to undermine the struggles of workers for a better life.

Primitive accumulation

One reading of economic history restricts the idea of 'primitive accumulation' to the early stages of capitalist development. This refers, for example, to the enclosures that established private property and forced rural people into the satanic mills in early industrial England, and to the high-seas privateering (piracy, really) that contributed to capital formation and helped to establish the Canadian banking industry. According to this view, the features of primitive accumulation that included brutal working conditions, slavery and child labor are identified with a bad old capitalism that has long since passed. Today, it is claimed, we have a sophisticated corporate version, a regulated and civilized capitalism that eschews bad behavior and operates in the interests of society as a whole. But while features such as child labor and piracy may have been modified – or at least displaced to countries such as Bangladesh and Somalia – new forms of primitive accumulation have taken their place. These stretch from the speculative derivatives market to privatizing the water we drink and the spaces we inhabit. The very notion of a public sphere has come into question, with the restless search for profit rendering the notion of public services and places an anachronism. A destabilizing market rationality is now in the process of penetrating every corner of our lives.

The features may have changed but the fundamentals of a recurrent primitive accumulation are still very much with us. As previously noted, capitalism still depends on the constant 'creative destruction' identified by Schumpeter during the Second World War when he wrote his classic *Capitalism, Socialism and Democracy*. Market enthusiasts are not apologetic about this destruction; rather the opposite – they identify it with the whole adventure of human progress. Without it, they believe, stagnation would ensue. One business school (the Rotman School at the University of Toronto) has even set up a Creative Destruction Lab to push the process along.[5] Creative destruction and its twin of heavy-handed primitive accumulation strategies tend to surface particularly when old avenues for extracting economic surplus begin to stagnate. A recent example was the situation when the post-World War Two consensus between workers, capital and government began to unravel in the 1980s. A period of relative prosperous stability based on decent wages and welfare provision for the sick, old and poor came under increasing pressure from corporations dissatisfied with their share of the economic pie. They advocated and funded a political program based on cutbacks, privatization, deregulation and other means of transferring wealth from labor to capital. This ran its course and these days the restless search for profit has shifted to the rather arcane region of the economy known as 'financialization'. The production of real goods and services now takes second place to speculative activity involving paper values and the rise and fall of stock and bond markets. Today, the value of the global derivatives market (bets on the future value of almost anything you can think of) is estimated at $1,200 trillion, which, it is generally agreed, is some 20 times the value of world economy.[6] This has been a fantastic source of profit for the small group of banks and related investment industries that dominate the global finance sector.

Needless to say, this can and does have a destabilizing effect on the overall economy. The speculative paper economy is in effect 'creatively destroying' people's livelihoods, forcing them to adapt to the brave new world of casino capitalism. The immediate losers here may be from the financial sector – although many of the top executives have a range of 'nest egg' strategies (tax shelters, niche real estate) that are available to all those with wealth. But the most profound impact is on the jobs and livelihoods of those who have no such means of protecting themselves. Even in the real economy, strategies of primitive accumulation can be destabilizing. Under globalization, for example, which is characterized by its proponents in the most glowing modernist language, economies previously based on industrial employment are being hollowed out as such work shifts to countries with cheaper labor. Youth unemployment and underemployment are soaring in the industrial world while wages and working conditions in the new industrial periphery resemble those in the early industrial revolution. Current primitive accumulation strategies have provoked a demand crisis, where stagnating incomes, combined with tight credit, are leading to long-term stagnation.

Neoliberalism

This current phase of capitalism is most frequently referred to as 'neoliberal'. This term has a wide variety of definitions and is used less frequently by its proponents (who prefer to speak of its

component parts, such as free trade, privatization, deregulation and investors' rights) than by its critics on the Left, who see it as a package of inter-related policies. If 'neoliberalism' is to mean something beyond a mere political swearword (reminding us of George Orwell's accusation that the epithet 'Fascist' was used too loosely back in the 1930s), it needs some more precise thinking. The notion of neoliberalism implies a return to the fundamental principles and philosophies that underpinned emergent capitalism. It implies rolling back the state, which is believed to be smothering initiative through a culture of dependence, and refocusing all policy initiatives according to market logic. But it involves far more than reducing state interference in the market to the levels of the pre-welfare-state 1920s. Embedded in it is a dangerously limited notion of the human that reduces us to mere calculators of individual economic costs and benefits. As one perceptive critic sees it:

> 'Neoliberalism... constructs individuals as entrepreneurial actors in every sphere of life. It figures individuals as rational, calculating creatures whose moral autonomy is measured by their capacity for "self-care"– the ability to provide for their own needs and service their own ambitions. In making the individual fully responsible for her- or himself, neoliberalism equates moral responsibility with rational action; it erases the discrepancy between economic and moral behavior by configuring morality entirely as a matter of rational deliberation about costs, benefits, and consequences. But, in so doing, it carries responsibility for the self to new heights: the rationally calculating individual bears full responsibility for the consequences of his or her action, no matter how severe the constraints on this action – for example, lack of skills, education and child care in a period of high unemployment and limited welfare benefits.'[7]

Neoliberalism in this reading, then, is about far more than

just re-installing the market at the center of the economy. It is a project that reduces all human activities to 'homo economicus' and takes in almost every sphere of life from criminal justice to immigration. Social policy is shaped to condition prudent behavior: workfare, pension reform to keep old people in the workforce, punishment of single-parent families, minimum sentences and other harsh criminal-justice measures. If you succeed, it is entirely down to your own efforts and your rewards should be bountiful and minimally taxed. You are a high-achieving 'rugged individualist' and don't owe anything to anybody. It is easy to see the appeal of this to CEOs with eight-figure pay cheques and the rest of the one per cent. If you fail, the responsibility also lies entirely on your shoulders for having 'mismanaged' your own life by making bad choices. You pathetic creature. No bailout for you. Government may help keep you alive if it doesn't cost too much but don't come crying for more than the bare minimum. You're lucky to get that. The underlying myth here is that all of us as citizens have an equal opportunity on a level playing field – so those that don't make it (an increasing number) must live with the consequences of their failures. Forget about class differences, inherited wealth, unequal educational opportunities, health handicaps and a profusion of other social factors.

Neoliberalism has become a sort of moral-rearmament political doctrine to accompany the market fundamentalism of economic policy. In these highly individualized economic circumstances, it is not surprising that the slogan that has become most popular with panicky voters during repeated election cycles is: 'It's the economy, stupid'. This captures the limits of government possibility as seen through neoliberal eyes – no room for compassion, intergenerational consideration, concern about the planet, international responsibility or democracy beyond the narrow confines of elections. There is simply no meaning outside the cold calculus of the market. This is also starting to undermine the institutions with which the establishment has traditionally been identified – the legal system, the police, parliament, local government. Under earlier forms of liberal democracy these could be counted on to play a moderately autonomous role in tempering capitalism. Under neoliberalism they are increasingly shaped so that they will not be obstacles to market priorities. Neoliberalism redefines democracy as market rationality – and the only criterion by which its political class can be judged is not principle but expediency.

Politically agnostic capitalism

The champions of the rule of capital (which they present as the rule of the market) hold forth that it is only capitalism that can deliver freedom. Market freedom is a precondition for all other kinds of freedom. Yet capitalism, with its market made up of a few winners and many losers, exists under all kinds of political arrangements – classical fascism (the Germany and Italy of the 1930s and 1940s), military dictatorship (the Latin American regimes of the 1970s and 1980s, along with so many others), feudal monarchy (Saudi Arabia), and now the state communism of China and Vietnam. The proponents of the 'capitalism equals freedom' point of view will hold that 'in the long run' the market will corrode such authoritarianism and freedom will flower. But, as John Maynard Keynes liked to say, 'in the long run we are all dead', and for the Saudi democrat the relationship between the House of Saud monarchy and petro-capitalism is all they can remember or even imagine. In Latin America, the overthrow of dictatorship led not to a capitalist renaissance but ultimately to various forms of populist socialism that are deeply suspicious of market forces.

Of course, to some degree it depends what you mean by freedom. The capitalist notion of freedom is all about opportunity. For the most part this means the opportunity (indeed the right, or even the obligation) of the individual to enrich themselves. This rather backward notion that you have the right to lord it over others because you are cleverer – or, more likely, better positioned due to the accident of birth – is another source of discontent with capitalism. Thoughtful people simply have the stubborn belief that we can do better than this. They have an underlying belief in the fellowship and solidarity of women and men and their capacity to co-operate with each other for the common good. Whether it is drawn from religious belief or secular conviction, or the experience of something better in their communities, families or memories, they just can't seem to get in sync with the rightwing US writer Ayn Rand's idea of selfishness as a virtue. They quickly come to realize that the opportunistic freedom of the derivative trader, real-estate speculator or arms dealer results in bankruptcies, evictions and corpses.

The second line of argument buttressing the case for capitalism as freedom of opportunity is that 'a rising tide lifts all boats'. This holds that the success of a few leads to the prosperity of the many through the creation of jobs and the famous 'trickle down' of wealth. You need look no further than the present state of the world, where inequality and the concentration of wealth are increasing virtually everywhere, to wonder at the sheer gall of those who hold this view. Around 0.1% of the world's population currently hold 50% of world income[8] and 51 of the world's 100 largest economies are now corporations.[9] In the meantime, rates of unemployment (particularly youth unemployment) are continuing to rise, imperiling the future of a generation.

All the same, opponents of capitalism have no right to be smug. The system has proved it has staying power. It has won at least the passive adherence of hundreds of millions of people who really have no significant stake in it. It has convinced them that there is no alternative but to play by the rules of capital's game. It has used crisis after crisis as a way of reinventing itself and opening up new avenues of profit. It has diverted scientific and technological progress to serve its own narrow ends. It has shown a flashy dynamism that still draws in the greedy and the gullible. It has undermined the alternatives that have been set up to oppose it, either through guile or force. It has appealed to what is worst in our natures, blinding us with celebrity and consumption (or at least dreams of future consumption). It has proved itself a worthy opponent and it is far from clear that capital can ever be brought to serve the purposes of humanity rather than the other way around.

For in the end it is not capitalists that control capital. They encourage it. Benefit from it. Obey it – or not, at their peril. But the history of business is dotted with ways in which capital has turned on them, driving them into bankruptcy, crisis, war or some other disaster. Many captains of industry and finance dwell under the illusion of their mastery of capital but it remains just that: an illusion. They have made a Faustian pact or devil's bargain and given capital its freedom to roam wherever it wishes, regardless of consequence. This is perhaps the most profound danger of capital on the loose in the current age: in its increasingly desperate quest for profit, capital is driving us over the ecological edge, endangering the very possibility of sustainable human life on the planet.

1 Daniel Cohn-Bendit, 'Enough with the European leaps of faith', opendemocracy. net 21 Mar 2013. **2** Jeff Madrick, 'US financial regulations; Plugging holes in a faulty dam', triplecrisis.com **3** Bob McGuire, 'Widening labour and peasant revolts threaten Chinese rulers', newsandletters.org Jan/Feb 2012. **4** Eli Friedman, 'China in Revolt', *Jacobin*, nin.tl/1fZplyj **5** rotmanventurelab.com **6** nin.tl/19D5vco **7** Wendy Brown, 'Neo-liberalism and the end of liberal Democracy' , *Theory and Event*, 7.1, 2003. **8** Capgemini and Merrill Lynch Wealth Management, 2009. **9** corporations.org/system/top100.html

3

State socialism

In practice, most alternatives to capitalism are seen as some form of socialism, which now has a checkered history stretching back over two centuries. The early stirrings of socialist thought eventually crystallized into two main forms: communism and social democracy, both of which are flawed and seem to have largely capitulated to the forces they once resisted.

'If you took the most ardent revolutionary, vested him with absolute power, within a year he would be worse than the Tsar himself.'
Mikhail Bakunin

Socialism organized through the state has been the main way in which humanity has tried to build an alternative to capitalism. We now have a couple of centuries of experience of this so it should be possible to build a balance sheet of positives and negatives. From the beginning, the state – or, if not the actually existing state, some idealized version of its socialist reformation – has been for most socialists a source of coherence and justice in opposition to the squalor and instability of the capitalist market. This view has drawn sustenance from the thinking of a wide variety of 18th- and 19th-century political philosophers, including Rousseau's notion of the 'general will' and Hegel's idea of the state as the high point of human rationality. The Left's allegiance to the state has been further reinforced by the unity of the state with the nation (the idea of the nation-state), which has allowed it the political luxury of dressing in the same patriotic clothes as the Right. While there have been competing currents of leftist opinion, it is this notion of a rational state as opposed to an irrational market that has until recently carried the day. This is the background needed for any understanding of what has been a largely uncritical view of the potential of the state to install and oversee a socialist alternative. The legitimacy of the political state and the way it exercises power remains one of the Left's major intellectual blind spots.

From its very beginnings there has always been a strain of socialism that has had about it an élitist and technocratic cast. This derives from its birth as a blueprint for reform issuing from the minds of social reformers such as the German activist and philosopher Ferdinand Lassalle and the French aristocrat Saint-Simon. Much of their politics was based on gaining access to the ear of those in power to convince them to implement schemes of social reform. Lassalle is credited with a certain amount of influence on Otto von Bismarck, one of Germany's most famous (and autocratic) chancellors, who laid down the beginnings of that country's welfare state. Other early socialist reformers, including the British factory manager Robert Owen, combined influence for progressive legislation with the establishment of utopian communities. Most such endeavors have had a slightly condescending attitude to the moral reform of wayward working-class personalities.

Another source of the original socialist impulse was popular movements of workers, particularly more educated craft workers but others as well, who saw economic democracy as an extension of radical republican goals. This tendency reached its first moment of decision at the time of the French Revolution, when there was a tension between a spontaneous revolutionary movement with radical egalitarian politics and its crystallization into a centralized political party in the shape of the Jacobins. It was the Jacobins who installed a dictatorship in Paris, supposedly to preserve and extend the revolution. They faced (or at least believed they faced) a tragic dilemma – how to preserve their revolution without betraying its radical democratic ideals. Arguably the Jacobins failed to do either. Since then, most revolutionary projects have been faced with a similar choice as to whether or not to be seduced by the temptation of deploying dictatorial means to impose social change from above. The Jacobin state under Robespierre used the citizens' army and the guillotine to dispatch those perceived as enemies of the revolution. In the end, the Jacobins created through such ruthless means the conditions for their own destruction, lashing out first against supporters of the *ancien régime* and then against radicals of the *sans-culottes* movement and other dissidents who were in favor of a more egalitarian republic. The Jacobins were left in a position of political isolation that set them up for defeat by the more moderate Girondins and ultimately allowed the rise of an emperor in Napoleon Bonaparte.[1]

This pattern reverberated through the revolutions of the 20th century. Lenin was inspired by the Jacobins when he created his own disciplined 'democratic centralist' Bolshevik party to spearhead the Russian Revolution. In doing so, he also created the dictatorial conditions that eventually condemned his Bolshevik comrades to death at Stalin's hand (although he didn't live to see it). Nemesis ruled, just as it did when Robespierre lost his head to the guillotine. With no freedom or power rooted in working-class society outside the Party, once the old Bolsheviks lost their power struggle to the ruthless Stalin there was nowhere for them to turn and they were murdered or executed.

Almost all revolutionary projects have been faced with this Hobson's choice in one way or another: either destroy their own revolution internally by the use of dictatorial means (Pol Pot's genocide in Cambodia is just the most dramatic example) or have it destroyed externally (as in Allende's Chile) by an alliance of powerful and ruthless enemies. Today, overt partisans of secular revolutionary dictatorship are rare – the odd Leninist or Trotskyist groupuscule, or mediagenic but politically isolated intellectuals such as the Slovenian Slavoj Žižek[2] or the French philosopher Alain Badiou. But these issues still haunt attempts to build a '21st-century socialism', notably in Latin America where the tension between democratic initiative and bureaucratic fiat remains – although at least now it is recognized as such and debated as never before.

Democratic roots in the 19th century

After their defeats in the French Revolution, partisans of an alternative to emerging 19th-century capitalism had a hard row to hoe. Throughout Europe, reactionary aristocratic and monarchical power did its best to smother or at least severely limit the democratic impulse. While economic space for business was allowed, political space – particularly the right of assembly and to form radical organizations – remained severely restricted. The goal of a socialist republic was, for movements of the Left, just the logical conclusion of the democratic dream. Some socialist theorists saw in these movements an agency for realizing political projects that could provide an alternative; they were increasingly aware that capitalism threatened the idea of a fully evolved democracy. Among their most treasured goals was the expansion of the franchise, given that the vote was then restricted largely to males with property. The main alternative in which those opposed to the system invested their hopes was a socialism brought about in one way or another through the democratic transformation of the state. In those days no-one doubted that the triumph of socialism meant more, not less, democracy. Opponents of socialism were staunchly opposed to such an expansion of democracy, seeing it as a form of threatening mob rule.

Along with other pioneers of socialism, Karl Marx saw the state as the fulcrum that could leverage a fundamental redirection of economic life. Marx, though, had very ambivalent feelings about the state. He thought of it as a transitional phase in the achievement of a stateless form of communism based on the democratic self-rule of producers. He was deeply suspicious of the bourgeois form of the state and saw a radical democratic transformation of it as a necessary precursor to socialism. For Marx, the Paris Commune, which saw leftists take over Paris between March and May 1871, was an example of the initial form of this socialist democratization of the state, with all its leveling features and directly democratic assemblies. His brilliant *Civil War in France*, which charted the ill-fated course of the Commune, was one of his finest pieces of writing.[3] This was the closest Marx came in his lifetime to seeing the self-emancipation of the workers to which he had dedicated himself.

In his writings on the state Marx chose to use the unfortunate phrase 'the dictatorship of the proletariat' to describe this transitional phase. The word 'dictatorship' had a far different and more limited definition in the 19th century than it has today. It meant a kind of directed control that would resist the challenges of the partisans of capitalism (particularly those that profited from the private control of the means of production) to reverse what Marx saw as a primarily democratic transition. But Marxism (not unlike the Bible and the Qur'an) can and has been used to support many different and competing viewpoints and interests. This is certainly true of the notion of 'the dictatorship of the proletariat' that was picked up by Lenin and other Bolsheviks to justify whatever draconian police-state measures they deemed necessary to protect their notion of socialism.

This blind spot about using state power to install socialism from above is common to the social democratic as well as the communist Left, and it has proved the undoing of the socialist hopes that were so strong in the 19th century. It has been consistently challenged by the advocates of change from below, be they anarchists or other libertarians of the Left. The debate has waxed and waned over the course of the last two centuries, with the 'practical' advocates of state power holding the upper hand for most of the time. However, the notion of an alternative from below has never entirely disappeared and, given the eclipse of the Leninist ethos and politics embedded in the communist world, it has become again the principal source of opposition to the tepid reformism of the center-left tradition.

Communism and social democracy

Few would today argue that over-reliance on a centralized state played a key role in the undoing of both the politics and economics of orthodox communism. The consequence was an alternative to capitalism that was decidedly unattractive, as it squeezed popular democracy and personal freedom while at the same time failing to deliver on the promise of economic prosperity. A highly centralized planning mechanism undermined any effective feedback from below on which to base decisions as to what and how much to produce. The result was a combination of shortages and oversupply that became a notorious feature plaguing state communist economies. The system was able to achieve a forced-march industrialization that enabled first the Soviet Union (and, much later, China) to survive in the face of aggression from Hitler's fascism and other enemies. A certain level of initial equality and security in daily life was eventually undermined by a growth in popular aspirations for a freer life with a wider range of opportunity and economic possibility. These systems have now been transformed back into a kind of autocratic capitalism where economic growth (spectacular in the Chinese case) has replaced stagnation but at the cost of galloping inequality. The usual, if limited, political freedoms associated with 'advanced' capitalism remain atrophied under these new forms of state capitalism. Undoubted advances in the general level of prosperity have not been accompanied by an opening up of the rights of assembly and independent organization that would allow trade unions and social movements to resist exploitation and inequality effectively.

In retrospect it could easily be claimed that orthodox state communism was not really an alternative to capitalism at all but merely a transitional form of it that allowed certain large 'backward' societies, hitherto blocked in their developmental path, to move towards their own peculiar model of autocratic capitalism. Today, both Russia and China, once the two centerpieces of world communism, have evolved into models of authoritarian capitalism in which a political élite, mostly made up of former communists, rules in alliance with a corporate and financial oligarchy. The ideological glue that sustains these regimes is no longer based on elusive communist ideals of equality or producer self-rule but instead on Great Power nationalism and individual self-enrichment.

The other strain of state socialism that has competed with orthodox communism is that of social democracy. This form of moderate socialism gradually separated itself from the (mostly European) revolutionary movements as it became a significant parliamentary force in the latter part of the 19th century. During the early years it rallied around issues such as trade-union rights and extending the franchise to include women and those without property – as has already been mentioned, in the 19th century it was almost always assumed by both proponents and foes that socialism meant greater democracy. The divisions on the Left were less about democracy than about the speed and scope of the necessary changes, and about whether tactics should involve direct action by popular movements or be restricted to elected representatives of the working-class movement fighting for reform in parliaments. While there were many who were critical of the parliamentary path (believing, not unreasonably, that electoral victory gave one the right but not necessarily the power to govern), the bloody defeats endured by revolutionaries gave the parliamentary argument a growing credence. Initially, those committed to the electoral arena claimed an almost slavish devotion to Marxist orthodoxy – Germany's Socialist Party theoretician Karl Kautsky was a classic example. But gradually there was a slippage as the give-and-take of parliamentary maneuvering and the difficulty of enacting reform in the face of bureaucratic and often military resistance led to a narrowing of political aims.

For the great social democratic parties of Europe (most prominently the German, French and British), World War One proved a watershed. Here was exactly the kind of conflict (a capitalist war fueled by nationalist posturing and the fight for markets and imperial influence) that socialism claimed to oppose. Yet party after party rallied around the flag, supporting a war that resulted in millions of young working-class soldiers dying or being maimed in the mud of the trenches. It was a shocking betrayal of the most fundamental socialist principles. The Bolsheviks in Russia, despite their increasing authoritarian tendencies, gained respect from socialists throughout Europe for their unflinching anti-war stand. Voting for the credits to fund the war became a kind of litmus test that shook up the world of socialists, provoking splits and resignations in many national parties. Anti-war activist James Ramsay Macdonald quit as head of the British Labour Party while the anti-war French socialist leader Jean Jaures was assassinated in 1914 by a militant French nationalist. The remaining leaders of the French socialists, including such previously uncompromising militants as Jules Guesde, were enlisted into the war effort.

This was the beginning of the end of the commitment of mainstream social democracy to spearheading the creation of an alternative to capitalism. Despite various ebbs and flows, the rest of the 20th century saw the drift of the Center-Left towards an inexorable accommodation with the capitalist system which is by now quite clear. The proponents of social democracy gradually abandoned Kautsky's adherence to Marxism in favor of a Keynesian growth model in which welfare spending was used to mitigate the inevitable inequalities generated by depending on the corporate-dominated market. The name of the game shifted from replacing capitalism to managing its business cycles and predatory nature in as fair a way as possible. Where national social-democratic movements tried to propose a more radical rupture with capitalism, they were brought to heel, usually by the market power of corporations and banks but also by the regulatory power of the International Monetary Fund, the World Bank and latterly the World Trade Organization. This was the fate, for example, of the Mitterrand government in France, which came to power with noble ambitions but in the unpropitious era of newly minted neoliberalism in the early 1980s (see below). Occasionally, in the case of particularly stubborn or popular socialist experiments, such as that of Salvador Allende in Chile in the early 1970s, it was necessary to use bullets or bayonets to bathe democracy in blood so as to discourage 'the irresponsibility of its people' (in Henry Kissinger's revealing words).[4] But, by and large, such embarrassing excesses were unnecessary as a tame Center-Left proved sufficiently accommodating to the needs of capital.

A tale of two social democracies

It is instructive to compare the government of François Mitterrand, whose Socialist Party formed a majority government in France in 1981, with that of Tony Blair's New Labour, which won three consecutive elections in the UK, starting in 1997.

The French Socialist Party has usually been more ambitious about reworking society than its British counterpart. Mitterrand entered government committed, at least in theory, to bringing parts of France's powerful financial and industrial sectors under public control. His government achieved some of this through nationalizations in its first years in power, while raising the minimum wage, adding an extra week of holiday, increasing pensions and other welfare allowances, and putting a solidarity tax on high incomes. By 1983 the government had run out of steam, with the franc being squeezed in order to keep it in the European Exchange Rate Mechanism (ERM, the precursor of the euro). France's currency was caught in the early vise of globalization, pressured by both financial speculators and the ERM. In addition, there was an investment strike by private capital that paralyzed the economy. The government made a *'tournant de la rigueur'* (austerity turn) that stopped the leftist program in its tracks with demands for labor flexibility and monetary and fiscal restraint. While some of the social gains proved difficult to roll back because of combative popular resistance, the publicly held industries were quickly sold back to the private sector at rock-bottom prices. The idea of a transition to socialism was abandoned, although Mitterrand continued to co-habit with alternating conservative and ever more tepid socialist governments for the full 16 years of his two-term presidency. A durable French nationalism replaced socialism as Mitterrand's main political coinage. In the judgment of one critic:

> *'The French events shatter the hopes or illusions that the transformation can be carried out gradually, without any break, within existing institutions, by purely parliamentary means, without the active participation of the people in their factories and their offices, without the unconcealed vision of another world indispensable to produce such a mobilization.'*[5]

The New Labour government of Tony Blair that took power in the UK in 1997 never presented itself as moving towards an alternative to capitalism – just the opposite. Blair and his intellectual mentor, the sociologist Anthony Giddens, worked to reposition Labour as a market, and business-friendly alternative to the 'destructive' class politics of both old Labour and the

Left in general. They called it 'The Third Way' and this term is sometimes also linked to the presidency of Bill Clinton in the US. The talk was of individual opportunity and a 'social investment' state that would allow those with initiative to rise, whatever their humble beginnings. New Labour language had an uncanny way of sounding like that of the neoliberal Right with its tendency to decry welfare dependency and to put much more emphasis on the obligations of the socially marginalized than on their rights. The idea was to leave the basic structure of the market-based economic process alone – though in fact the neoliberal project started under Margaret Thatcher in the 1980s was speeded up through further deregulation and privatization. Social spending (and not a little coercion) were to be used to enable those previously left out to participate in the wonderful opportunities that globalized capitalism would provide. It was in 2006 that Tony Blair and his circle theorized this into what he called 'a new social contract' based on the notion that 'we grant each citizen a stake in our society but demand from each clear responsibilities in return'.[6] This is language reminiscent of the Clinton and Obama administrations in the US. It is quite clear throughout that it is up to the authorities to delimit your rights and to decide when your responsibilities have been carried out properly. It is also a neoliberal departure from the old world in which you used to have the gall to believe you had some entitlements as a citizen. No welfare without being willing to take dead-end jobs. No hip-replacement surgery without weight loss. No right to demonstrate without police approval of routes and times.

It turned out that the responsibilities to be undertaken outweighed the opportunities that were on offer, and the inequalities that plagued British society were largely unaffected by New Labour policies. But the one thing that should be said of New Labour is that it set a new standard for unapologetic bluntness among political parties of the Center-Left. There were no illusions with Blair and company that there was going to be anything but an embrace of actually existing capitalism with a bit of tinkering at the edges. It is the prototype of a new kind of social democratic party that has abandoned any significant attempt to reform capitalism and adopted 'enlightened' neoliberal policies. Its resilience can be seen in its echoes elsewhere – particularly in the German Social Democratic Party under Gerhard Schröder. Their efforts are geared to convincing a disheartened electorate that they are the most efficient managers of capitalism. Social justice is off the table and has been replaced by modest taxation and balanced budgets.

Capital's modernizers

Today's center-left parties vary greatly. Few have gone (at least publicly) as far as the UK's New Labour in their complete commitment to capitalist modernity. It is fair to say, however, that almost all now present themselves in one way or another as modernizers of capitalism rather than as positing an alternative to it. Their aim is to shave off the rough edges by making the system fairer and better thought out. They underestimate the power of corporate actors to manipulate and undermine whatever 'rules-based' economy they envision; they underestimate the essential irrationality and instability on which this 'most radical of all social systems' thrives; and they underestimate the sheer inertia built into the structure of the state – a kind of in-built conservative bias that derails their chosen vehicle of reform. They also ignore the myriad ways in which the state is tied into the capitalist power structure – or else simply accept these as the inevitable price of political realism.

Achieving high government office becomes a question of compromise and careers. It tends to trap the Center-Left into managing the fundamentally undemocratic structures (including the security apparatus) of government, and this sucks all the oxygen out of any remaining social vision. The state in an advanced capitalist society is hemmed in by the sheer weight of the corporate economy on which it depends for the fundamentals of economic well-being: growth, taxes and jobs. This gives the corporate élite serious weight (often presented as a subtle form of blackmail) when it comes to blocking any kind of alternative or even regulatory tinkering that they feel will threaten corporate power and prerogatives. Globalization, of course, greatly enhances the capacity of capital to move its resources around the world when threatened. This is no paper tiger, to use Mao Zedong's phrase. Only a radical government with a significant counterweight rooted in society would have any hope of facing down such forces. But instead of building this kind of counterweight, the Center-Left concentrates on organizing to gain and keep electoral power. It remains trapped in a parliamentary political culture where achieving snail-like incremental reforms is the cause of much self-congratulation. The very things that it criticizes elsewhere in the political culture – hierarchy, short-sightedness, a politics tuned to the news cycle, leadership through personality rather than program – also shapes its own behavior.

The problem of the state

It is the state that, in different ways, has consistently derailed socialist ambitions. In its Bolshevik form it led to dictatorship and the inevitable degeneration into ruthlessness and corruption. Cynicism at the top resulted in a cynicism from below reflected in the bitter political humor that proved such a popular escape valve in communist society. Take the old Hungarian political joke: Question –'What is the difference between capitalism and communism?' Answer – 'One is the exploitation of man by man and the other is the opposite'. Once concentrated in dictatorship, political power can never be effectively dispersed. It is the one drug for which there will never be prohibition.

For socialists, the state has therefore proved more of a problem than an opportunity. It is less an instrument than a terrain on which (often vastly unequal) forces engage in struggle over the direction of policy and the allocation of scarce resources.[7] Public-service unions, the nuclear industry, the universities lobby, the financial sector, small business, welfare-rights organizations, the environmental movement, the armaments industry: all duel over this piece of public turf. It is a terrain in capitalist society that is starved of resources by inadequate and unequal tax systems and so becomes the 'wasteful' whipping post of the political Right. The Right presents itself as some kind of faux anarchism, mobilizing people's disappointment and attacking 'politicians' while aspiring itself to take political power. This is a game in which the Center-Left has become hopelessly enmeshed: losing any sense of how to turn the oil tanker around, it has eventually decided that it is not possible or even desirable to do so.

Even the libertarian Left, with its more thoroughgoing critique of power, tends to lose its way when it comes to the state. Libertarians are more likely to become obsessed with state power as an instrument of evil rather than one of potential good, to caricature the scheming state by reducing it to its most repressive apparatus. It tends towards conspiracy theories and its imagination runs to barricade politics and apocalyptic revolt. While not necessarily wrong in its focus on the repressive nature of power (particularly when trying to defend the right of assembly against police forces who regard it as simply an excuse for troublemaking), extrapolating this into a view of the state as a whole is ridiculous. Many functions the state has been forced to take on (mostly due to partial victories won by pressure from below) are of benefit to people and society. Denouncing (as opposed to critiquing) public healthcare, environmental regulation, old-age pensions, health-and-safety legislation, consumer protection and free education is bound to strike most potential supporters of a politics of anti-capitalism as absurd.

In some ways classical anarchism has the same narrow, instrumentalist view of the state as do the proponents of state socialism. The failure to adopt a more sophisticated view of the state continues to narrow emancipatory politics and to reduce its potential. It seems unlikely that the state's arbitrary power can ever be destroyed by direct assault in the streets. As Kurt Vonnegut, that iconoclastic voice of North American letters, remarked in one of his essays: 'There are two main reasons for working within the system – tanks and machine guns'. The political state of the 21st century has invested a huge amount of wealth into its repressive capacities and is well positioned (one could argue eager) to resist a frontal assault of militant anti-capitalists or anybody else.

A more promising avenue is that an extended battle on its own terrain has at least the possibility of shifting the focus and dispersing the power of the state. This will involve rethinking democracy to build a counterweight to the priorities of the corporate economy. The political class will continue to be an obstacle in this process and any hopes that attach to their more populist members as far-seeing 'representatives' of anti-capitalist transition will likely lead to disappointment and demobilization. The institutional power of the state itself needs to be recast and re-rooted back into the society it so badly represents.

1 Daniel Guerin, *Class Struggle in the First French Republic*, Pluto, 1977. **2** Slavoj Žižek, *In Defense of Lost Causes*, Verso, London, 2009. **3** Karl Marx, *The Civil War in France: The Paris Commune*, reissued by International Publishers, London, 1989. **4** BBC News, nin.tl/16gPTLn **5** Daniel Singer, *The Meaning of Mitterand*, Oxford University Press, Oxford, 1988. **6** *The Guardian*, nin.tl/Hc2VAi **7** An early example of examining the state as a terrain can be found in James O'Connor, *The Fiscal Crisis of the State*, Transaction Publishers, New York, 2001.

4

The anarchist impulse

Anarchism as a political doctrine did not take shape until the 19th century but the impulse behind it has much deeper roots. The split between libertarian thinkers and state socialists proved costly, contributing to the dead end of Soviet communism. But anarchist influences have made a strong comeback in recent protest movements worldwide.

'Anarchism is democracy taken seriously.'

Edward Abbey

The desire not to be subject to the arbitrary authority of others and to captain your own ship is as old as recorded memory. Capitalism has used this universal desire to cloak itself in a libertarian guise by proclaiming that the freedom of the market is the only realistic way to achieve this more general freedom. But this cloak quickly shreds for most people as the growth of corporate monopoly usurps economic and eventually political power – and as their labor activity (most of their waking hours) is reduced to a commodity to be bought and sold and subject to the profit-seeking whims of a boss. Despite capitalism's pretensions to the contrary, the anti-democratic scars on our everyday lives are pretty obvious. From its early days, capitalism's claim to represent the only realistic human freedom has been challenged by anarchists and other libertarian currents who have always said a resounding 'no' to arbitrary political and economic power.

Those sympathetic to anarchism have searched in both history and anthropology for the ancestors of more recent anarchist thinking and movements. What they have found are examples of uncompromising revolt and a passion for self-rule that dot human experience back to the days of our predecessor species *Homo erectus*. It would be dishonest to call this 'anarchism'. It is rather evidence that the instinct for revolt and the desire for self-government are rooted deeply in the human psyche and historical experience and, for some anarchists, this provides confirmation that they are on the right track. Anthropologists have found much evidence of hunter-gatherer societies both past and present that share these tendencies. The Iroquois Confederation of northeast North America was, for example, a fairly well elaborated attempt at such self-government. Similarly indigenous influences –including notions of sharing wealth and of a sustaining earth (*Pachamama*) – in places like Ecuador and Bolivia continue to help shape attempts to create contemporary libertarian alternatives to capitalism.

Some anarchists – including the Russian noble Pyotr Kropotkin – saw the Neolithic village as a mostly peaceful and self-governing community before the formation of the state and predatory armies started to wreak havoc. Ancient and medieval history offer up plenty of examples that were often elaborate in their aspirations but partial in their achievement – Greek city states, slave revolts against Imperial Rome, monastic communities, heretical sects in revolt against religious authority, agrarian agitators – all swam against the tide of arbitrary authority. Two figures who stand tall in historical memory are Thomas Müntzer, a leader of the peasant revolts in Germany in the early 16th century; and Gerrard Winstanley, an inspiration of the Diggers movement that defended the Commons at the tail-end of the English Revolution in the mid-17th century. Winstanley in particular recognized authority and property as a deadly combination that undermined popular liberty.[1]

The organized anarchist movement

The roots of formal anarchism can be traced back to the revolutions of 1848 when Europeans tried to overthrow the despotism that had held the continent in its grip since the defeat of Napoleon Bonaparte – that wayward child of the French Revolution. In 1848 a contagion of revolt spread across Europe – and not only where one would expect it, in revolutionary Paris, but also in such previously unimaginable locations as Vienna, which had long been under the brutal boot of Metternich's Habsburg Empire, and Berlin, which had been subject to the whims of the Prussian aristocracy. From Palermo to Prague, it was the kind of year that resembled the more recent experiences of 1968 or 1989 when the spent ideologies and prerogatives of the old order came up for challenge by minds as well as feet and fists. The end of the year saw dashed hopes, slammed jail cell doors and too many corpses as the powers that be took their pound of flesh. In Paris thousands were executed without trial or even examination.

But the immediate political failures should not conceal the fact that 1848 was the birth date of many of the most long-lasting alternatives to capitalism, including anarchism. The two pioneers who defined the early days of the movement were Mikhail Bakunin from Russia and Pierre-Joseph Proudhon from France. Both had been marginal participants in 1848 and had witnessed the betrayals and compromises of the middle class that laid the ground for a working-class radicalism inspired to go beyond the usual republican demands. It was Proudhon, an autodidact socialist from the Jura region of eastern France, who first coined the word 'anarchist'.[2] In a prolific lifetime of writing stretching from his first *What is Property* (from which comes his ringing rejoinder 'property is theft') to his final *The Political Capacity of the Working Classes*, Proudhon tirelessly advocated a decentralized and mutualist society that was sharply distinct from the Jacobin centralism that he saw as the Achilles' heel of the French Revolution. For Proudhon, a kind of federalism was the best political form through which the working class could achieve autonomous self-rule. His solutions to society's problems were often practical and he (like Karl Marx) resisted laying down elaborate blueprints for the future and was highly critical of the utopian political thinkers who did so. Proudhon's influence remained after his death and can be traced from the Paris Commune and the First International to Mexican agrarian radicalism and the US radical syndicalist IWW (The Industrial Workers of the World or 'Wobblies'). His reputation has, however, been sullied by his reputed defense of patriarchy and by accusations of antisemitism.

The colorful Mikhail Bakunin, oldest son of a minor Russian noble family, was very different in temperament and outlook from the measured and thoughtful Proudhon. He was less of a theorist and more of an agitator and pamphleteer. Bakunin was a bear of a man with enormous appetites and energy. He wandered Europe involving himself as an organizer in revolts from Dresden to Bologna. His politics were apocalyptic and his temperament mercurial, both of which traits were captured in his uncompromising phrase, 'the urge to destroy is also a creative urge'.[3] He served sentences in some of Europe and Russia's worst prisons before escaping and fleeing across the world – only to return to Europe's barricades. He started as a pan-Slavist conspirator to free the Slavic nations from the yoke of Tsarism and other autocracies. But by 1863 he had largely abandoned this cause in favor of organizing groups advocating an international anarchist revolution to overthrow the capitalist state. His influence expanded, particularly in southern Europe and eastern France, until he brought his groups into the First International, where he did battle with Karl Marx over the orientation of the anti-capitalist movement. His anarchist contingent was eventually expelled by the more statist communists, although the influence of anarchism remained firmly rooted, particularly in southern Europe. Irascible to the last (many questioned his sanity), he died in July 1876. Bakunin was a man of the grand gesture who had apocalyptic visions of working-class freedom, but his anarchist politics were somewhat tainted by a taste for conspiracy and a belief in a murky 'invisible dictatorship' that would install the perfect society.

In classical anarchism as represented by these two giants there exists an internal tension between the idea of an evolution of libertarian tendencies and practices within society and a notion of violently overthrowing power through acts of mass defiance. One can trace this tension through every manifestation of the libertarian movement, whatever the social and geographic context. Anarchist thinkers right down to the present have fallen on either side of this divide, although the tendencies in favor of violent overthrow have lost ground in the face of the overwhelming power of the modern state with its ruthless security apparatus. On the insurrectionary side have been such figures as the Italian Enrico Malatesta and the working-class-based anarcho-syndicalist movement, which reached its high water mark in Spain's CNT union and North America's Industrial Workers of the World.

On the side of a more gradualist approach to building the spaces and practices of self-rule so as to challenge state structures were figures such as the Russian geographer Pyotr Kropotkin, whose books – particularly *Memoirs of a Revolutionist, Mutual Aid* and *Fields, Factories and Workshops* – were tremendously influential in spreading anarchist thought. After being imprisoned in Russia and France, he was granted asylum in London, where he did much of his writing and influenced such figures of British radical letters as Bernard Shaw, Oscar Wilde and William Morris, as well as currents of non-statist thought such as Guild Socialism. His anarchism tended towards nonviolence and his influence was large, spreading even to India where Mohandas Gandhi adapted Kropotkin's thinking to his own notion of a village-based libertarian society. After 1917, Kropotkin returned to Russia but found himself out of sync with Lenin's Bolshevism – he was publicly critical of the Cheka police-state measures employed by the Bolsheviks. When he died, in 1921, his funeral procession through Moscow's streets was five miles long, carrying both anarchist and socialist flags – this represented one of the last libertarian protests against the autocratic course the Russian Revolution was taking.[4]

After the failures of 1848, the anarchist movement underwent significant growth, particularly in France and the Slavic and Mediterranean countries. This was not just a question of a few isolated intellectuals but significant sections of working-class opinion, as with the watchmakers of the Swiss Jura or the workers from the marble quarries around the Italian town of Carrara. The continuing popularity of anarchist thinking could be seen clearly in the revolt of the Paris Commune in 1871, when the city rose against an enfeebled government, outraged by its failure to stop Prussian aggression. The influence of Proudhon and the anarchists far outweighed any other socialist current, including that of Marx, who famously saw the Commune as the first example of working-class self-government.

Ebb and flow

After the defeat of the Commune, the anarchist movement dwindled to near invisibility. Indeed, as the anarchist writer George Woodcock often pointed out, the history of anarchism is one of recurrent ebb and flow.[2] He sees a resurgence of libertarian thought and organizing again in the 1900s, with an ebb following the anarchists' defeat at the hands of Bolshevism (1917-1922) but another flow in the 1930s, when classical anarchism reached its high water mark in Cataluña and Andalusia during the Spanish Civil War. The Spanish trade-union confederation, the

CNT, whose two million members underpinned the Republican side in the Spanish Civil War, was anarcho-syndicalist in its orientation. Woodcock believes that, while there are historical correspondences between these different waves of anarchism, they were also shaped by very different contexts. He is not alone in seeing libertarian thought as vital to the formation of the international New Left in the 1960s. New Left notions of participatory democracy had much more of a libertarian than a Leninist ring to them. Although Woodcock never lived to see it, he would undoubtedly have recognized the influence of anarchism and other libertarian strains on the global justice and Occupy movements that animate current radical opposition to ever more dubious forms of capitalism.

The Left is well known for its various splits and fissures. To some degree at least, this is because ideas and principles matter more than expediency in socialist culture. Perhaps none of these splits have been as momentous (and unfortunate) as two that took place at the end of the 19th century. In 1872, at a conference of the First International in The Hague, Marx and his allies expelled the anarchists who rallied around figures like Bakunin, Malatesta and James Guillaume of Switzerland. This event not only tragically split the forces of the Left but allowed for the evolution of more authoritarian strains of communism without the check of libertarian radicalism.

The second fateful split came to a head in 1896, when the libertarian delegates were expelled from the International Socialist Congress. Principled socialists such as William Morris and Keir Hardie opposed the expulsion but for most social democrats the libertarian criticisms of electoral opportunism and 'practical' politics had become just too irritating. The consequences here were as profound as that of the earlier expulsion. Within a generation, bureaucratism and capitulation had become so rife in social democracy that the parties lost their souls by rallying around their respective national flags in the slaughter of World War One. These parties also had a record of supporting the colonization policies of the European empires amongst the 'lesser races' of Asia and Africa. Without voices to raise doubts about the corruptions of conventional politics and state power, social democracy was gradually transformed from an alternative to capitalism to a more humane version of its management.

A broader libertarian impulse

It was not anarchists alone who foresaw and reacted to the problems of top-down power. Within the broader socialist movement voices started to be raised that were critical of both Bolshevism and social democracy for their willingness to use autocratic or conventional state power as the main means for implementing socialist measures. These included Paul Lafargue (Marx's son-in-law) and William Morris, who challenged the orthodoxies not only about the state but also about the nature of work and the purpose of economic growth.

The seminal figure to emerge as an advocate of a radical but libertarian socialism was, however, Rosa Luxemburg, who was a leader of the left wing of German social democracy. An adroit thinker and dedicated activist, she was quick to realize what would be the ultimate consequences of Bolshevism's dogmatic interpretation and application of Marx's 'dictatorship of the proletariat' in the Soviet Union. She engaged in political battle on all fronts. She was critical of the capitulations of the center of German social democracy. She also regretted the autocratic Bolshevik short-cuts that undermined the fledgling power of the Russian working class, which had blossomed in the Soviets (workers' councils) of 1917. But her hardest struggle, one in which she lost her life, was the workers' revolt in 1919, which challenged the Junker class that had led Germany into the slaughter of World War One. Luxemburg was murdered after she was betrayed by her former comrades on the right wing of the German Social Democratic Party.

The failure of socialist transformation in post-war Germany in many ways isolated the Russian Revolution, ensuring that its worst potential overcame its best. Nevertheless, the period after the First World War in Europe was one of great intellectual and political ferment, where people dissatisfied with a world that allowed their young to be slaughtered in the trenches sought something new. One form this took in western Europe was the workers' council or council communist movement, which engaged tens of thousands of workers in places like Germany, the Netherlands, Italy, Hungary and Britain. Among its leading lights were Anton Pannekoek in Holland and Sylvia Pankhurst in the UK. Many invested their hopes in these councils as a kind of radical direct democracy that could be the basis of a new society. The movement's failure to achieve its goals, due to a combination of internal division and ruthless suppression, forestalled the development of a libertarian alternative to the top-down communism of the Bolsheviks. Other notable and innovative thinkers of the time were György Lukács in Hungary and Antonio Gramsci in Italy, though both of these in the end made an uncomfortable peace with orthodox communism.

The history of the libertarian Left after this is rich in its diversity but poor in its record of political accomplishment. While there were many mimics of Lenin's democratic centralism and later of Chinese Maoism, those that privileged a democratic yet radical approach to building an alternative to capitalism remained on the margins of political culture in most countries – at least until the Left sought to reinvent itself in the 1960s. Among the currents that kept the embers of libertarian thought alive during the long dark night of Stalinism in the East and 1950s post-War conformity in the West, was the Paris-based group Socialisme ou Barbarie (whose animating spirit was the Greek political thinker Cornelius Castoriadis). Another was a group of Detroit-based activists called the Johnson-Forest Tendency, which included the remarkable CLR James of Trinidad and Raya Dunyayevskaya of Sri Lanka as well as the Chinese-American Grace Lee Boggs.

By the 1960s, the prospects for a libertarian alternative to capitalism appeared much brighter. The state socialist competition that had outstripped anarchist and other libertarian currents was looking distinctly threadbare. The Soviet model was running out of steam and various bursts of enthusiasm for Chinese Maoism proved short-sighted and short-lived. Student movements were challenging the hierarchical nature of both capitalism and state socialism. The flavor of the times was caught in the title of a short but widely distributed polemic by the Franco-German student leader Daniel Cohn-Bendit – *Obsolete Communism: the Left Wing Alternative*.[5] Cohn-Bendit and his fellow theorists of the New Left were reviving the traditions of libertarianism and advocating a militant but pragmatic approach for the future. It was the beginning of the end for Leninism as the default position in radical leftist political culture.

The 1960s and 1970s saw an amazing flowering of different forms and perspectives for those seeking a way out of capitalism. The anarchist impulse was felt again by many but without the legacies of loyalty to the old-school traditions of the movement. It became somewhat less of a doctrine and more of a sensibility. Libertarianism informed the critique of conventional politics in the early US-based Students for a Democratic Society notion of a 'participatory' rather than simply a 'representative' democracy. The French revolt of 1968, which was influenced by anarchist and situationist currents, brought forth great intellectual imagination in teasing out the big issues in crafting an alternative to capitalism. The Parisian intelligentsia put on the table such issues as the urban and its spaces as a site of insurgency (Henri Lefebvre), the morality of power (Michel Foucault) and the interaction of ecology and politics (André Gorz). The Italian New Left contributed the notion of 'autonomy' in the 1970s, with special emphasis on the need to rethink such things as the hierarchical structure of work and political organization. The shortcomings of the various movements of the time and their failure to reach the ambitious goals they set for themselves should not blind us to the innovation involved in breaking the old molds of left thinking. Old orthodoxies were challenged in a way that would ensure they could never again be taken up with the same reverence. Frustration and defeat led some movements back into the search for old certainties (various forms of Maoism and Trotskyism resurfaced and still persist) but they proved short-lived dead ends.

Another nail in the coffin of state socialism and the Bolshevik tradition occurred after the collapse of the Soviet Union and the overthrow of unchallenged Communist Party rule in its former satellites between 1989 and 1991. Not that most of these societies embraced other forms of socialism – just the opposite, in fact. After years of line-ups and shortages, and desperate for the consumer cornucopia that capitalism had come to represent, there was little appetite for thinking about alternatives. A couple of decades later, now that the insecurities of life in the market system have struck home, the tenor of politics is much darker than the sunny optimism of the immediate post-Soviet era. A modest rebirth of the Left has, by and large, been eclipsed by various strains of authoritarian nationalism, fueled by a desperate search for a stable identity amid the shifting sands of the global market economy.

The end of classical anarchism?

There has, however, been a substantial rebirth of libertarian sentiment as part of the Left's resistance to the globalization of capitalism from the mid-1990s. The global justice and Occupy Wall Street movements have drawn inspiration from a range of different influences, as libertarian traditions have fused with more modern influences such as the Mexican Zapatista movement and ecological radicalism. While the old Bolshevik-inspired sects still exist on the sidelines, the main thinking about alternatives to capitalism is decidedly decentralist – encapsulated in the 'one no and many yeses' pluralism first advanced by the Zapatistas.

The classical anarchism that did battle with Marx and the state socialists may be disappearing. The old doctrines of anarcho-syndicalism and 'propaganda by the deed' seem somewhat archaic in this era of mass depoliticization and eco-collapse. In their own way, anarchists too have believed in the Enlightenment notion of Progress with a big P. Murray Bookchin's notion of a post-scarcity anarchism, with its glorification of a liberatory technology, is but one example – which, in fairness, Bookchin himself came to question.[6] Maybe the real victory of anarchism is not in the triumph of large (if decentralized) organizations, bravery on the barricades or exposing the machinations of the deep state. Perhaps it lies more in the diffusion of a libertarian resistance to authority throughout society, particularly in modern social movements.

A good example here is the rise of the feminist critique of male power and how it is exercised. Feminism has its anarchist roots, of course, in Emma Goldman, an early and persistent champion of women's emancipation and critic of the sexual slavery she associated with patriarchy.[7] Goldman was followed by such libertarian feminists as the Russian Alexandra Kollontai, who was (at least initially) critical of the top-down authority of the Bolsheviks. The growing acceptance and assertion of women's rights has eliminated or at least significantly challenged a large amount of arbitrary power over the lives of both women and men. But it has gone beyond the informal and personal to raise questions as to the legitimacy of how political power is exercised through the state. Feminism in its more radical manifestations has deepened the critique of instrumental power (generally wielded via the state by men) and posited a more local, self-affirming notion of power exercised through broad community participation. British feminism was particularly strong in its exploration of this area, influenced by women like the historian Sheila Rowbotham and the activist Hilary Wainwright, who both tended to see their feminism as part of a more general social transformation. Rowbotham drew out some of these links in a 2011 interview:

> *'...the emancipatory individualism of the subordinate, which I think is really important. It's also been part not only of the women's movement but of movements around race and class where there is always that aim of self-realization and self-assertion, because that's what's being denied these groups by the powerful. But this is different from saying, "I'm only concerned about myself and my own self-interest".'*[8]

This libertarian strand of feminism is obviously not the only brand out there – other feminist doctrines are more preoccupied with helping powerful women climb the institutional ladders of economics and politics to break the 'glass ceilings' that have long frustrated careers and ambitions. There is also the kind of feminism that turns to the authoritarian state to control bad male behavior. But it is by no means clear that these forms of feminism result in any significant or long-term change in the exercise of arbitrary power on either gender.

There are a number of other ways in which libertarianism has been set loose as a subversive influence with the potential to undermine the capitalist command system (as exercised through corporations and their political servants). Social movements exist within a broader milieu of 'civil society', which includes a number of non-state actors, such as non-governmental organizations, that advocate for the broader public interest and often act as watchdogs on state power. Perhaps the presence of some of the militant and uncompromising offspring of classical anarchism can act as a check to challenge civil society when it drifts in too statist or 'professional' a direction.

1 Kenneth Rexroth, *Communalism: From its Origins to the Twentieth Century*, Seabury Press, New York, 1974. **2** George Woodcock, *Anarchism and Anarchists: Essays*, Quarry Press. Toronto, 1992. **3** nin.tl/17pWQwy **4** nin.tl/1cggzfT **5** Daniel Cohn-Bendit, *Obsolete Communism: the Left Wing Alternative*, Penguin Books, London, 1969. **6** Murray Bookchin, *Post-Scarcity Anarchism*, Wildwood House, London, 1974. **7** Emma Goldman, *The Traffic in Women and Other Essays on Feminism*, Times Change Press, New York, 1971. **8** *The Third Estate*, nin.tl/17pXryj

5

The eco-divide

Not so long ago, the environment was taken no more seriously by the Left than by the Right. But the mounting evidence of ecological crisis has forged a new dividing line in politics – between those who insist on business as usual, whatever the costs, and those who understand that all of us, all over the world, have to find new ways of living within our ecological means.

'When the forms of an old culture are dying, the new culture is created by a few people who are not afraid to be insecure.'

Rudolf Bahro

Before the 1960s, most of the alternatives to capitalism shared many of the same basic assumptions as the capitalist system itself. This common set of received truths that ran from right to left across the political spectrum included shared notions about the value (indeed absolute necessity) of economic growth, a concept of progress dependent on the exploitation of the supposedly endless bounty of the natural world, and an almost unqualified belief in the beneficial nature of science and technology. The gospel of progress that had been born in the Enlightenment was widely believed and the future of humanity was thought to depend on 'the conquest of nature' providing the good life. Division came over how this was to be brought about – through the state or through the market, by the bourgeoisie or by the proletariat, and so on. Many critics of capitalism saw the central issues in dispute as being to do the distribution of wealth and power. Karl Marx himself, in most of his writings, particularly the later ones, was of the view that qualitative growth in human development and the full-blown application of science and technology were being blocked by a capitalism that was dependent on the profit motive and the social relations that flowed from it.

There are ecological socialists – John Bellamy Foster among them – who champion the notion that Marx was an environmentalist from the outset, at least by implication. This view holds that Marx explored a 'metabolic rift' that capital had opened up between humans and nature.[1] Undoubtedly such thoughts can be found in Marx but they co-exist with a celebration of material progress as the path to human advancement. Communism would be built on the plenty achieved by capitalist industrial expansion. Such a view lent itself to the idea of a passive nature acted on by active human labor. Marx was not alone among 19th- and early 20th-century critics who put their faith in a productivist model of society where a central priority was for humans to shape nature in a way that could provide fairly for the entire species. If there were environmental 'irrationalities', such as pollution or the over-use of resources, it was assumed that such phenomena would disappear more or less automatically once capitalism had been eclipsed. If such issues were dealt with at all, they were seen to be side issues of minor importance compared to the core struggle of the classes over distributing the spoils of economic activity.

There were, of course, a few discordant voices who put greater emphasis on the ecological quality of the alternative to capitalism, and who did not assume some post-scarcity land of plenty once capitalism had been transcended. Such thinkers as the Russian libertarian geographer Pyotr Kropotkin foresaw the need to put an end to a society based on the domination of nature. The English socialist William Morris was a voice in the wilderness due to the centrality he gave to ecological decay and its connection to a society based on 'useless toil', to which he was diametrically opposed. He was one of the few socialists who were not advocates of full employment as a precondition of any socialist future but instead saw the reduction of work as a key socialist demand.[2] He saw such a reduction as a precondition to the evolution of a healthy society where labor would be measured by its contribution to ecological sanity. The anti-work theme – encapsulated in Marx's son-in-law Paul Lafargue's famous pamphlet *The Right to be Lazy* – was usually associated with a critical attitude towards productivist society.[3] Rethinking work – particularly using jobs as the main means of distributing income – has in recent years become an important part of most ecological visions of an alternative to capitalism.

The rise of environmental consciousness

With the gradual birth of ecological consciousness – landmarked by the publication of Rachel Carson's 1962 classic *Silent Spring* on the effects of agrochemicals and the 1970s debate over limits to growth – a profound unease about the assumptions underpinning our productivist society has been gathering momentum.[4] Is the widespread use of chemicals in industry and agriculture poisoning our own habitat and that of other species? Is our dependence on non-renewable resources and their rapid depletion putting us in a position of running on empty – peak oil, peak uranium, peaks of several types of minerals? Are we turning what should be renewable resources (soil, fish, water, forests, even air) into rapidly depleting non-renewable resources by 'mining' them with heavy technologies (building mega-dams and draining aquifers; using trawler fleets and drift nets; allowing agro-chemical runoff, soil compaction and desertification; clear-cutting forests)? Is our dependence on carbon endangering those who live in coastal areas, river valleys, or other habitats vulnerable to extreme weather and other consequences of a global temperature rise?

These questions loom increasingly large, casting a shadow over not only capitalism but any orthodox alternative to it. The dismal communist record on the environment can been seen in the dried-up Aral Sea between Kazakhstan and Uzbekistan, the radioactive protection zone still surrounding the Chernobyl nuclear reactor in Ukraine, and the looming water and energy crisis in China. Under communism, the triumphalist Stalinist mega-project – redirecting rivers, huge hydroelectric dams, soulless high-rise apartment blocks – were the *sine qua non* of progress. The collapse of the Soviet bloc actually slowed global climate degradation, at least temporarily, as dysfunctional polluting industries went to the wall. Today, only Cuba, with its emphasis on alternative energy and organic agriculture, stands as a partial alternative to sacrificing the environment on the altar of economic development – and even there it is not clear if ecological initiatives are being carried out through conviction or due to necessities imposed by a Soviet collapse and a US embargo. Only time will tell. Elsewhere, as with the late Hugo Chávez crafting a form of petro-socialism in Venezuela, short-term advantage seems to be trumping long-term ecological sanity. The history of the post-colonial Global South is marked by nationalist governments, often describing themselves as socialist, that champion development no matter what the ecological costs.

Greening of the Left

An ecologically coherent Left must come to terms with its own productivist roots if it is going to mount a convincing critique of capitalism. The need for an alternative is urgent, as capitalism is irredeemably committed to a form of growth that endangers the existence of human life on Earth. But, to find it, the Left must recreate itself by reorganizing around a program of eco-sanity and challenging a process of growth that is not only moving too fast but also in a clearly unsustainable direction. It is by now pretty obvious that both inequality and growth are built into the very DNA of the capitalist system. Capitalism can never be about selling us less, living in a more modest way, or reducing inequalities so as to allow us to share within our own societies – let alone the planet as a whole – in a sustainable fashion. The 'me first' ethics that underpin consumer culture are in sharp contradiction to the mutuality needed if we are to find a collective way to live more lightly on the earth.

The most visible political manifestation of the rise in ecological consciousness has been the birth of Green parties that now populate parliaments and assemblies around the world. These started with the German Greens and have managed to get a toehold in many countries, particularly where electoral systems are organized around the more democratic system of proportional representation. The first-past-the-post system popular in the Anglo-Saxon world has been successful in marginalizing Green political representation.

Green parties have been around now for several decades so it is possible to draw up an initial balance sheet of their successes and failures. From being a voice in the wilderness, they have progressed to the stage of occasional participation in government, albeit very much in a minority position. While often able to act as an environmental conscience and to have some influence over legislation, they have not been immune to the careerism and horse-trading that dominate the electoral arena. They tend towards an ideology of pragmatism based on the somewhat facile claim that Greens transcend the politics and issues that divide left and right. They are often plagued by having to make the same kind of compromises that have seen the Center-Left adapt itself so readily to the needs of managing a capitalist economy. In short, they are torn between the vision of a more ecological society and maintaining their precarious foothold influencing the major political players to pass incremental environmental reforms. Tensions similar to those on the social-democratic Left have sprung up between official Green parties and an impatient set of environmental social movements and organizations. It is fair to say that, since the early debates between the 'realos' and 'fundis' within the German Greens, Green parties have avoided positing themselves as any kind of overall ecological alternative to capitalism. This has left them prey to dubious notions such as 'green growth' and 'green jobs' to prove their case, which at worst can be seen as a superficial greening of the growth coalition – effectively an attempt to sustain the unsustainable. This has also allowed them to be painted into a corner as a single-issue party of 'tree-huggers' who have little to say about the overall organization and direction of society.

The German Greens (*Die Grünen*) have been by far the most successful Green party, and their deterioration in terms of vision and principle speaks to the heavy price paid for adapting to politics as usual in exchange for often ephemeral or surface-scratching reforms. Once the flag bearer of a challenge to the overall direction of industrial society, *Die Grünen* are now reduced to a bit part as a minor power-broker in conventional German party-political bargaining. They have been seduced by ideas of eco-efficiency and green capitalism in order to position themselves on more comfortable center-left ground. Radical currents have either left or been expelled and the mechanisms of direct democracy and radical accountability have been sacrificed on the altar of 'maturity'. Most shockingly of all, several of the best-known Green political figures (including former Federal foreign minister Joschka Fischer) have become paid lobbyists for a range of corporate sectors, including the pipeline, nuclear, pharmaceutical and even tobacco industries.[5] The corruption of personal ambition and the enticements of power should never be underrated in political cultures that trade on such things.

Beyond growth politics

A more basic challenge to the overall direction of capitalism and the social and ecological wreckage it is piling up is essential. Just a few basic facts are sufficient to show that the current desperate search for new sources of growth is heading us towards oblivion. First, the rate of increase in growth (as measured by GDP) across the industrial world has been declining or stagnating (depending on the country) for decades. There are no signs of significant recovery – just the opposite. So it makes good sense to seek a different measure for our economic well-being aside from growth. Second, the negative impacts of the growth fetish, both ecological and social, are accumulating to a frightening extent. We would need 4.1 planets to consume and pollute if the whole world lived at the rate of US citizens (about 2.5 planets at the rate of the French). [6]

In his sober assessment of the 1972 ground-breaking study *The Limits to Growth* (a book greeted with much skepticism on the Left when it came out), the journalist Christian Parenti shows that, 40 years on, *Limits* got a lot right. While taking issue with some of *Limits'* arguments about the running out of resources, Parenti holds that, on its second major theme, the limits of natural sinks to absorb growth-generated pollution:

> 'The Earth's capacity to absorb the filthy byproducts of global capitalism's voracious metabolism is maxing out. That warning has always been the most powerful part of The Limits to Growth. Most worryingly, we have overloaded the atmosphere with heat-trapping CO_2 and, in recent years, discovered that the sea has also absorbed vastly more carbon dioxide than was thought. As a result, the ocean's average pH level is about 30 per cent more acidic than it was 100 years ago. This is threatening the formation of calcium carbonate exoskeletons in shellfish, including the very tiny ones at the base of the marine food chain. In other words, lots of the fish we eat, like salmon,

rely for food on these acidity-threatened little creatures.'[7]

You could explore a range of other issues – such as soil and fresh water degradation – and arrive at similarly alarming conclusions. Of course, it is true that the ecological footprint is badly skewed in favor of the wealthy. It would take a number of fair-sized African villages to have the same ecological impact as one upper-middle-class multi-vehicle-owning family commuting into New York or London from the affluent suburbs. Inequality is the other major consequence of skewed capitalist growth. The Occupy movement, protesting against the one per cent and its lightly taxed paper wealth, is just the latest symptom of disenchantment with such obscene disparities. It is here that red and green preoccupations can rub up against one another in an uncomfortable fashion. For those of an eco-socialist persuasion, it is essential that the costs of slowing growth are borne in an equitable manner. This means that the basic needs of all populations must be taken into account and the reductions associated with diminished growth possibilities, whether planned or unplanned, be applied first and foremost to those with an opulent lifestyle. It is easier to imagine this happening if degrowth takes place in a thought-out fashion rather than through an unplanned application of 'lifeboat ethics' that allows the powerful to protect their privileges while the vulnerable go to the wall. But have no doubt – degrowth there will be! It is just a question of whether this will result in equitable and democratic social arrangements or in gate-guarded communities serviced by underpaid workers and surrounded by large populations of environmental refugees.

Dividing the pie is a stereotypical metaphor often used to separate supporters of capitalism from those who want something better. It goes something like this: a conservative would accuse a socialist with being obsessed with how to apportion the pie, whereas he or she would be more concerned with making it bigger. But what if making the pie bigger is no longer on the table as a realistic option? Mainstream economists such as Robert Gordon of Northwestern University, echoed by Paul Krugman writing in the *New York Times,* now believe that the age of growth that started in the 18th century is drawing to a close.[8] This growth has always been fueled by a combination of technological innovation that provides lucrative work and abundant free (or at least cheap) ecological goods. Both these conditions are changing. Ecological goods (clean air, good soil, pure water, carbon and mineral resources, fish) are becoming scarce and/or expensive while the revolution in computer technology has failed to provide widespread lucrative employment. Indeed, it has been a major contributor in shifting wealth from labor to capital and aggravating inequality both between and within national borders. But, while economic growth has stalled, resulting in social disruption and resistance, particularly in southern Europe, the momentum towards what that doyen of social science Robert Heilbroner feared as 'an ecological Armageddon'[9] is still gathering pace. The connection between climate degradation and extreme weather events is becoming increasingly difficult to deny. In such areas as global warming, species extinction and oceanic health, we appear to be reaching global tipping points.

Vivir bien

Any alternative to capitalism needs a post-growth future. There are by now many strains of Left ecological thinking trying to hammer out just what this might look like. There are the beginnings of a degrowth movement: this started in France and Spain and is now spreading to North America. There is a social ecology movement inspired by the writings of Murray Bookchin. There have been several attempts to fuse the socialist tradition with environmental concerns. Political theorists James O'Connor and John Bellamy Foster have explored such a synthesis in their writings. These are being underpinned intellectually by the burgeoning field of ecological economics, led by such notables as Herman Daly and Joan Martinez-Alier, as well as by a mounting body of climate and other environmental science that continues to reveal the deadly trajectory of the current growth obsession. From the Global South comes an indigenous perspective based on the defense of Terra Madre, which has become a competing tendency within the Latin American Left. Elsewhere, movements of resistance in Africa and Asia are working to defend the survival economy on which the rural poor depend by standing against deforestation, in defense of watersheds and in defiance of mega-projects designed to fuel various 'economic miracles' built on sand. The notion of a different, more equitable, development strategy has long been a counterfoil to the globalizers' obsession with GDP growth. It has by now reached the point that any alternative to capitalism which does not accord the ecological survival of humanity a central place in its program simply cannot be taken seriously.

The post-growth alternative to capitalism needs to be different in its very language. It must move beyond earlier preoccupations with class struggle, while maintaining its commitment to equality and democracy. It must come to terms with ideas such as overshoot, carrying capacity, ecological footprint and tipping points in order to help shape a fair and sustainable future. It must find new strategic perspectives that do not rely on the centrality of the rapidly disappearing industrial working class in Western countries. It is faced with the task of welding together a movement from very diverse sources and places but with enough commonality to be a powerful influence in shaping an equitable future based on ecological democracy. One such source is the notion of 'living well', which is rooted in the traditions of the indigenous Andes and has gained some traction with the Bolivarian movements of Ecuador and Bolivia.

'*The Constitutions of Ecuador and Bolivia are the most well known in their reflection of these ideas; the first presents the idea of "Good Living" or Sumak Kawsay (in Quechua), and the second, "Living Well" or Suma Qamaña (in Aymara). Similar notions (although not the same) exist in other indigenous cultures, such as the Mapuche in Chile, the Guaraní in Bolivia and Paraguay, the Kuna in Panama, the Achuar in the Ecuadorian Amazon, and in the Mayan tradition in Guatemala and Chiapas (Mexico), among others.*'[10]

This idea, which in Spanish translates into *vivir bien*, has echoes around the world in a more nature-friendly and convivial mode of sustainable living – in different ways, this same spirit can be felt in the slow food movement, in degrowth initiatives and in many other expressions of 'living well', and can be opposed to the accelerated consumerism of possessive individualism. In its most political expression, *vivir bien* is contrasted to conventional notions of development with their dichotomies of domination: society/nature, advanced/backward, center/periphery, wealth/poverty, and so on. It is a tool for overcoming the oxymoronic notion of 'sustainable development', which has become a kind of 'all things to all people' formula for justifying corporate growth. This is just one of many possible starting points for building an ecological democracy – and the notion of degrowth is one that we will explore more deeply at the end of this book.

1 John Bellamy Foster, *Marx's Ecology: Materialism and Nature*, Monthly Review Books, New York, 2000. **2** William Morris, *Political Writings*, Lawrence and Wishart, London, 1973. **3** Paul Lafargue, *The Right to be Lazy*, Kessenger Publishing, 2009. **4** Rachel Carson, *The Silent Spring*, Houghton and Mifflin, New York, 1962. **5** Joachim Jachnow, 'What's Become of the German Greens?' *New Left Review*, May/June 2013. **6** nin.tl/1eKTXIW **7** Christian Parenti, 'The Limits to Growth; A Book that Launched a Movement', *The Nation*, 5 Dec 2012. **8** nin.tl/1h0wZzb **9** nin.tl/19SsVL0 **10** Sumak Kawsay & Alberto Acosta, 'Ecuador: building a good life', 24 Jan 2013, upsidedownworld.org

6

The utopia debate

Utopian thinking is liable to provoke scorn from all sides – and totalitarian blueprints have given it a bad name. Yet conservatives are as prone to dream of perfect free markets as radicals are of equality or living in harmony with the Earth. Utopias are not watertight models but rather visionary arenas for debate that help us approach a better, fairer world.

'We can only know what we can truly imagine. Finally what we see comes from ourselves.'

Marge Piercy[1]

The history of different imagined and desirable futures is longer than that of the current epoch of capitalism through which we are suffering. Arguably, utopian thinking goes back at least to Plato's notion of an enlightened oligarchy ruling over his Republic. Thomas More gave popular birth to the word with his own vision of a utopia located on an island in the Atlantic Ocean. The degree to which such futures were or were not utopian (and whether this was or was not a bad thing) has been a cause of sharp disagreement among critics of capitalism. Karl Marx was particularly scornful of utopian thinking among the socialists that preceded him, such as Charles Fourier and Robert Owen; he counterposed his own socialism, which he claimed to be scientific. Despite Marx's prestige in the socialist movement, there continued to be utopian speculations in the writings of William Morris, Edward Bellamy and a number of anarchist thinkers. But, by the time of the Russian Revolution, it was widely believed by socialists of nearly all stripes that a more practical socialism had gained ascendancy and that the utopian variant had all but vanished from the field. Ideals gave way to the exercise of power.

But history plays some strange tricks. Conventional state socialism has proved a disappointment even for many of its adherents, who were often among the first to proclaim its outright failures. It is now Leninist communism, which once inspired millions, that is no longer a serious alternative for most people. At the same time, women and men have never really given up dreaming of what a better world might look like. Such dreams have helped fuel criticism of the shortcomings of what came to be known as 'actually existing socialism' as well as of social democracy. These visions have come from various sources, including artistic avant-garde movements such as surrealism, which tried to integrate Freud's notion of unconscious desire into a revolutionary project, and, more recently, situationism (associated with Guy Debord and the Situationist International), which influenced the insurgent movements of 1968 and after. In the first surrealist manifesto, penned back in 1924, André Breton proclaimed that 'to reduce the imagination to a state of slavery is to betray all sense of absolute justice within oneself. Imagination alone offers me some intimation of what can be.'[2] Many utopians have used literary fiction as a way of exposing their readerships to potential future worlds. More recently, anarchist (Ursula K Le Guin), feminist (Marge Piercy) and ecologically inspired (Ernest Callenbach) utopian writers have started using science fiction for this purpose.[3]

The anti-utopians

Keeping utopian thinking out of politics has united both the conventional Left and the conservative Right. They have worked hard not only to disparage its unrealistic nature but also to paint it either as a dangerous kind of adventurism (the Left) or a sinister form of terrorism and/or totalitarianism (the Right). Both criticisms have been used to foreclose debate and protect current institutional set-ups from the probing questioning they so badly need. Other critics have insisted that we face 'the facts' – that we live in the best of all possible worlds and that only slow incremental change is desirable or, indeed, even possible. For the wave of traumatized intellectuals escaping pre-World War Two Europe as refugees – Karl Popper, Isaiah Berlin, Friedrich Hayek, Hannah Arendt and so many others – any vision of radical change was hemmed in by nightmarish probabilities. They had a profound influence, particularly on social science in the Anglo-Saxon world, which quickly spilled over from academia to infect the political class and the media. It is, of course, fatuous nonsense to brand all humanistic utopian visions as stalking horses for Nazism or Stalinism. But it has become an intellectual staple of the *status quo* that any radical utopian proposition takes us down the road of authoritarian imposition at best or to the killing fields of Kampuchea or some kind of crazed jihad at worst. In a conservative sleight of hand, however, many reactionaries still hold a soft spot in their hearts for the 'perfect competition' utopian writings of the rightwing libertarian Ayn Rand. It clearly depends whose utopia we are talking about.

In reality, utopians have been at least as much the persecuted as the persecutors. Utopian communities have often been treated with suspicion and utopian thinkers disparaged or imprisoned. Back in the 15th century, the Italian utopian philosopher Tommaso Campanella was tortured and suffered life imprisonment for his idiosyncratic views.[4] There are many,

many other examples. And, while the quality of utopian thinking varies widely, in most of it there is simply a refreshing desire for a more equal and inspiring way of life. It is more often animated by a gentle humanism than by sinister design. This is from Thomas More's original *Utopia*, published back in 1516, half a millennium ago:

'In all other places, regardless of the prosperity of the country, unless the individual takes care of his own needs, starvation will be his fate. This self-preservation has priority over the common good. Here... no-one ever lacks anything. There is no begrudging the distribution of goods, poverty and begging are unknown, although, possessing nothing, all men are rich. For who is richer than he who lives a happy and tranquil life free from the anxieties of job holding and domestic troubles?'

More touches a sensibility that could help us build the kind of post-growth future currently so necessary to our own survival as a species: an ecological democracy that takes the individual off the consumer treadmill and revalues the quality of daily lives. Much other utopian speculation tends to this kind of peaceful radical egalitarianism. However, when utopians stray into providing detailed schemes for how the future should be organized, they tend to get into choppy water. The devil is in the detail, as they say, but when it comes down to categorizing a hierarchy of types of citizens and their purpose, as Plato does in his *Republic*, or the color and type of clothing that women must wear, as the German Christian utopian Johannes Valentinus Andreae did for his imagined community of Christianopolis, it is no wonder that people begin to become nervous.[6] Marx was probably right in his reluctance to speculate on the details of life under communism, thinking that, in history, utopias write themselves. Still, after a century and a half of trying none too successfully to hammer out a viable alternative to capitalism, a middle course between micro-managing the future and buying a pig in a poke may be necessary. If those proposing an alternative to our current capitalist civilization can only say what they don't want, and cannot give us a sense of what they actually propose, success will likely remain elusive.

One of the recent defenders of the utopian tradition is the Californian historian Russell Jacoby, who has written extensively on the subject. When he published *The End of Utopia* in 1999, he was distinctly pessimistic about the future of the kind of utopian thinking he believed was essential to revitalize stagnant mainstream politics. He felt the universal ideas embedded in most utopianism were being drowned by post-modern relativism. He famously proclaimed that 'once students dreamt of healing the ills of society; now, based on the students I have, they dream of going to good law schools'.[5]

A lot has happened since the publication of *The End of Utopia*, with the rise of the anti-globalization and Occupy movements, and a series of grassroots world and regional social summits that have re-invigorated critical thinking about possible futures. The chickens have also come home to roost for the capitalist expansion unleashed in the Thatcher/Reagan neoliberal revolution of the 1980s. What started off as a get-rich-quick speculative boom has now turned into a bust that has shattered popular faith in the system, as various miraculous investment bubbles from high tech to real estate have burst, one after another. This seems to be a fertile time to rethink our social and economic relationships. Indeed, much of this is already happening. Jacoby's other shortcoming is that he does not pay much attention to the environmental crisis, which urgently demands an imaginative recasting of humanity's relationship to nature. In his second book on the subject, *Picture Imperfect*, Jacoby makes the useful distinction between blueprint utopianism, which lays out the future in painful detail, and what he terms idiosyncratic utopianism, which champions more open-ended possibilities.[7] The former arouses his skepticism, while he sees the latter as a kind of essential freethinking about alternative futures.

Whatever the merits of a particular utopia, none are in any way acceptable to partisans of the current capitalist *status quo*, with its market religion that needs to be defended with whatever authoritarian measures prove necessary. For a conservative, the most irritating thing about utopians is that they always want to return to first principles. The unquestioning belief held by the dominant political class is that first principles should just be assumed to be embedded in our current way of life – the glorious heritage of our noble ancestors having been won by some heroic (usually military) struggles of the past. If this is not taken as an article of faith, it opens the door to all kinds of speculative and destabilizing questioning. Is our democracy really democratic? Do we really have equality of opportunity? Can we not find a better source of social cohesion than individualistic self-promotion? Is our current obsession with growth compatible with the ecological survival of the human species? Is it fair for some people to starve while others live on billions of dollars worth of inherited wealth? Current statistics reveal that the 300 wealthiest families in the world possess more than the total wealth of the poorest three billion people.

It is easy to see why such questions are a source of potential subversion or at least significant embarrassment for those with power and prerogatives to defend, who find it far better to dismiss such speculations as idle daydreaming and to debunk any attempt to rethink our current social arrangements.

The utopianism of the powerful

It is not entirely clear, however, who are the realists and who are those bewitched by some promised land just over the horizon. There is at least one school of thought which holds that the mainstream of Western thinking itself – from the monotheistic religions coming out of the Middle East, through European enlightenment notions of progress, down to present-day capitalist rationality and market fetishism – is forever pointing towards a future that never seems to arrive. This is the utopianism of the powerful. Secular progress has replaced celestial reward for a life of good works. You are now motivated to scrimp and save for that dream home, latest electronic gadgetry or jet-set lifestyle. It is the consumer carrot rather than the stick of the fiery furnaces of hell that compels obedience. Even Marxism, with its belief in a classless New Jerusalem, can be seen as just another future-centered project where present sacrifices and struggles will be rewarded by a scientific socialist version of 'pie in the sky'.

In the present era, the distinction between the religious notion of salvation and the secular promise of progress has become quite blurred. Religion, particularly muscular fundamentalist Christianity (but also political Islam), is merging with a belief that human salvation lies in technology and progress realized through the market. The early slogan of General Electric was 'Progress is our most important product' and the corporate legal theorist William Cook maintained that 'laws of commerce are stronger than the laws of men'. Kenneth Lay, the failed Enron CEO, declared: 'I believe in God and I believe in markets.' Such views are commonplace among the captains of commerce. For the Hungarian political economist Karl Polanyi, the idea that 'the laws of commerce were the laws of nature and consequently also the laws of God' was in effect 'a blind faith akin to the fanaticism of sectarians'.[8]

According to this utopianism of the powerful, the dystopian difficulties of the present are simply evidence of the sacrifices we make on the altar of some eventual salvation. It is replete with biblical imagery, with shifting ideas as to who gets to play the 'chosen people' and what ethos they must employ to reach their preferred promised land. The American frontier; the Argentinian pampas; the African veldt; the 'True North'; even outer space: all have had their turn to play Israel in this quasi-biblical metaphor. The displaced may be Palestinians or indigenous peoples or anyone standing in the way of the march of colonial armies and the extractive promise of corporate initiative. There are wildernesses to conquer and savages to subdue – all 'for their own good', we are assured. Yet somehow it is always those who don't have to make sacrifices who demand them of others.

All this salvationist belief is inspired by the idea of a *telos* or goal that is held to be embedded in human history – God's will (be it a Jewish, Christian or Islamic one), the forward march of progress, the inevitability of communism, the perfect competition of the marketplace. The travails of the moment are imbued with meaning by this goal – the suffering of the poor can be redeemed by hard work, religious faith, political self-sacrifice or by apocalyptic rupture with a sinful past. In the present 'common sense' utopia, the multitudes are all encouraged to aspire to a boundless consumer bounty inspired by the American Dream. This remains (and will always remain) an elusive, if glittering, goal for most of humanity, who have no hope of ever achieving it. Those who have at least a small bite of the apple are under constant threat of having it yanked away by the insecurities that inevitably accompany capitalist development. The 2008 mortgage crisis in the US put paid to the home-owning dreams of tens of thousands. The sovereign debt crisis of 2010 has undermined the security and aspirations for material prosperity of millions across the Eurozone and elsewhere. Meanwhile, inequality grows and hundreds of millions across the world barely survive on a couple of dollars a day.

But even if all could share in the dream of consumer bounty, it would quickly turn into an ecological nightmare as the global resources needed to sustain it simply do not exist. As the slogan goes: 'There is no Planet B'. But, after all, who doesn't want the latest computer game or phone with an app that can cook your dinner for you? Two of the most eloquent critics of this seductive materialist salvationism are Frederick Turner, whose *Beyond Geography* is a powerful indictment of Western civilization's despoiling of the wilderness,[9] and David Noble, whose short classic *Beyond the Promised Land* creatively captures the sweep of human history and its distortions by generations of self-interested priests and hucksters. Noble believes that today 'the mythology of the promised land [has become] gospel truth, in the form of common sense "market solutions", free trade agreements, computerized utopias and genetically engineered salvation and the inevitability of globalization – as well as the resurgence of religion itself.'[8]

A lived utopia

But in opposition to the seekers of the promised land, be they religious or secular, there has always been a current of thinking that has celebrated life as it is in the richness of everyday life and has seen through the cant of salvationist morality as the cloak of self-serving élites. These thinkers have looked to the humane values of community solidarity and empathy with a more rooted morality than the grand abstractions and expediencies of nation and profit. Their attitude has been to defend existing rights and common spaces against the modern enclosure movement of privatization and the grand narratives of human destiny. It is tempting to turn the tables, as Noble tries to do, and to see such resistance as being grounded in a strictly anti-utopian perspective. But it is far from clear that the examples he cites, from the Zapatistas of southern Mexico to the anarchist and autonomist movements that are the core of the resistance to globalization, are all opposed to re-visioning the future: rather the opposite. The post-Seattle slogan 'Another world is possible' is in itself evidence to the contrary.

It is pretty clear that those who want to build an alternative to capitalism cannot help but think about what that alternative is going to look like. The warning that arises out of the utopia debate is that we need to be pretty careful about how this is done. Make your utopia open-ended and non-dogmatic, not some 'terminal point' in history where all human suffering disappears. Avoid being glib. Eschew grand abstractions like the unfortunate 'dictatorship of the proletariat'. Steer clear of detailed blueprints or techno-fantasies. But explore grounded possibilities of how people's lives could and should be better. How can people lead more secure and psychologically rooted lives? How can new social arrangements be put in place to overcome the restless destabilizing nature of capitalism with its attendant insecurities? How can we distribute the world's wealth in such a way as to guarantee a decent level of equality? How can democracy be something more than popularity contests amongst the political classes? How can our working lives become something more than dead time controlled by others? How can we live lightly on the earth in order to sustain ourselves and the natural world on which we and other species depend?

We are bound to identify elements of what is occurring in the present as anticipating what might be in the future. Thus, for example, the collapse of the permanent employment economy could presage more democratic and less compulsory forms of work. Or the evolution of civil society and social movements could anticipate a form of self-governance closer to the ideal of democratic self-rule than our current limited forms of political representation. It is also worth remembering that at one time such causes as ending slavery, child labor or the eight-hour day were thought of as utopian dreams that would never be achieved.

The German philosopher Ernst Bloch took a kind of idio-syncratic utopian stance and was a source of inspiration in the 1960s for both European radicals and the liberation-theology movement that shook the Catholic Church. Although by no means a believer in blueprints, his work *The Principle of Hope* is considered a classic utopian text for the modern era. He talked about 'fermenting in the process of the real itself', by which he meant a 'concrete forward dream: anticipating elements are a component of reality itself.'[10] Bloch died in 1977 but he surely would have recognized some modern developments – the Latin American attempt to recraft a socialism for the 21st century, for example, or the defense of the commons against market predators that is sprouting up almost everywhere – as 'prefigurative elements' of a different potential future.

There have been a number of recent imaginative yet practical attempts to sketch what a possible alternative future might look like. Michael Albert's *Parecon: Life After Capitalism* is one; others are André Gorz's *The Critique of Economic Reason* and Alec Nove's *The Economics of Feasible Socialism*.[11] These vary widely in their perspective but are a breath of fresh air in an era when market fundamentalists continue to insist that there is no alternative but more and more of the same. These alternative thinkers are divided on a number of important points: participation in economic decision-making (Albert) versus some form of social market (Nove) being a vital one. But the differences might help us more in our quest for the right balance than some blueprint platform fantasy handed down from on high. The Brazilian popular educator Paulo Freire could not imagine life without an animating sense of utopia: 'what is not possible, however, is to even think about transforming the world without a dream, without a utopia, without a project.'[12] Without visions, we will sink into what Bloch feared most – a state of toxic dreamlessness. It is here that the crackpot realists and their line that 'there is no alternative' would have us reside.

1 Marge Piercy, *Woman at the Edge of Time*, Knopf, New York, 1976. **2** André Breton, *Excerpts from the First Manifesto of Surrealism*, mariabuszek.com **3** Ursula K Le Guin, *The Dispossessed*, Harper & Row, 1974; Piercy, op cit; Ernest Callenbach, *Ecotopia*, Banyan Tree, 1975. **4** nin.tl/1ahJrRC **5** Russell Jacoby, *The End of Utopia*, Basic Books, New York, 1999. **6** Claude J Summers, *Fault Lines and Controversies*, University of Missouri Press, 2002. **7** Russell Jacoby, *Picture Imperfect: Utopian Thought for an Anti-Utopian Age*, Columbia University Press, 2007. **8** David F Noble, *Beyond the Promised Land: The Movement and the Myth*, Between the Lines, Toronto, 2005. **9** Frederick Turner, *Beyond Geography: The Western Spirit Against the Wilderness*, Rutgers University Press, 1992. **10** William K Carroll, 'Crisis, Movements and Counter-Hegemony', in Henry Veltmeyer (ed), *21st-Century Socialism*, Fernwood Publishing, Halifax, 2010. **11** Michael Albert, *Parecon: Life After Capitalism*, Verso, London, 2003; André Gorz, *Critique of Economic Reason*, Verso, London, 2011; Alec Nove, *The Economics of Feasible Socialism*, Allen & Unwin, London, 1983. **12** Paulo Freire, *Pedagogy of Indignation*, Paradigm, Boulder, 2004.

7

Rebuilding the alternatives Southern-style

In Latin America, many countries are experimenting with forms of '21st-century socialism' that are charting new ground. All over the world, communities dependent on land, forest and water sources are fighting to defend them from corporate exploitation. And the old idea of 'the commons' as a resource for all may yet provide us with a new way forward.

'The biggest challenge is to get people who are commoners to realize that they are commoners.'

Saki Bailey[1]

It is beginning to happen in parts of the Global South. In Latin America there is an attempt to reinvent a '21st-century socialism' that empowers the grassroots rather than being imposed from above by the state. In the Muslim world, the Arab Spring, despite its mixed results, has created the desire for a deeper democracy that goes beyond the normalization of religious and economic privilege. Almost everywhere, 'defending the commons' has become a rallying cry for those defending the ecosystem and its resources from privatization for profit, removal from popular control and ultimately destruction.

Movements to create an alternative are more resilient in the South, perhaps because the stakes are more obvious. The shrouds of ideology that blanket political culture in the North are thinner and more tattered here. It is not so easy to throw around words like 'the market', 'democracy' and 'national security' and expect people to take it all at face value. Sure, even in the North not everyone is fooled – eyes glaze over, shoulders shrug and people make rude jokes. But in the South people are swifter to anger. Quicker to take to the streets. Less afraid of the authorities. Less willing to give those 'above' them the benefit of the doubt. This is partly a consequence of popular experience. When they've tried everything on you, including torture and murder, what do you have to lose? Their lies become obvious. Disinformation is assumed to be the rule rather than the exception. Desperation breeds courage. But there is also a canny sense of what hasn't worked before and the need for experimentation – a quarry of popular experience.

Of course, it is possible to be romantic about this kind of resistance. Repression often works. Fear is real. Death is final, at least for those who die. People everywhere can always be tricked by the bogeys of religion, tribe, nation or whatever other imagined 'dark force' is held to be their mortal enemy. But fear in the Global South has a different quality, being focused on power and those who wield it. We in the North, meanwhile, tend towards a more depoliticized response, fearing abstractions like chaos and insecurity. It is harder to deal with such intangibles when crafting a politics that tackles business as usual head on, yet this crafting is exactly what needs to be done. In the South, the political nature of exploitation and who is benefiting from it is usually a lot more obvious. The politics of resistance can be misconstrued or misguided but the retreat into a privatized apathy is a lot less likely. This chapter looks at

Southern attempts to build alternatives to capitalism in much less depoliticized circumstances.

21st-century socialism

The phrase '21st-century socialism' was given weight and immediacy by the Bolivarian movement set in train by the late Hugo Chávez in Venezuela. This movement, which aimed to use the country's oil wealth more for the benefit of the poor, has found ready echoes in many other parts of Latin America as the continent has, over the past decade, moved substantially (if unevenly) in search of alternatives to the Washington Consensus. This 'Consensus' had held sway until the late 1990s and was based on the usual notions of giving free rein to international capital through policies of free trade and investors' rights in the (mostly unfounded) belief that this would create stable employment and 'trickle down' prosperity. The Consensus was reinforced with US military aid to the region, including the training of corps of rightwing military officers to make sure that a politics supportive of these policies stayed firmly in place.

Latin America has a long and bloody history of oligarchic rule and revolt against that rule. From Simón Bolívar, liberator of the continent from Spanish colonialism in the early 1800s, to the Mexican Revolution in the early 1900s; from the movements of Augusto Sandino in Nicaragua in the 1920s and Juan Bosch in the Dominican Republic in the 1950s to the stubborn revolution in Cuba from 1959 onwards: from Salvador Allende's ill-fated Chilean experiment in democratic socialism in the 1970s to the Sandinista challenge in Nicaragua in the 1980s: the river of revolt runs deep in Latin American history. From the Argentinean Pampas to the drylands of northern Mexico, the marginalized and exploited of the continent have never taken their lot in life lying down for long. But their attempts to free themselves have often been met with the kind of ruthless class oppression that leaves stomachs empty and bodies in the street. Some of these failures and limitations were at least to a degree self-imposed by the Left – the corruption of the Sandinistas in Nicaragua and the refusal of Cuba's revolutionary leadership to democratize their socialism. But far more significant was the constant attempt to teach the Left and its supporters one final bloody lesson. It was this that motivated military despots such as Chile's Pinochet, Guatemala's Ríos Montt and a plethora of others. It is a history to be both mourned and celebrated, and no-one does it better than Eduardo Galeano in his poetic history of the region, *The Open Veins of Latin America*.[2]

This history of repression is not ancient. Bloody dictatorships, backed and sometimes even installed by the United States, smothered democracy in favor of Washington Consensus capitalism throughout the 1970s and into the 1990s. Tens of thousands died for merely trying to exercise rights that *gringos* have long taken for granted. Chile under the Pinochet regime became a kind of neoliberal model to be bandied about by its US sponsors for other Southern countries to emulate. In this exemplary autocratic paradise, the only real freedom was that given to private capital to go wherever its investment inclinations led. It was a model that enshrined inequality, in a region which, measured by the Gini Index, was already the most unequal in the world. From the days of the conquistadores' first land-grab, there has always been good reason for Latin Americans to sing along to that 1920s show tune *Ain't We Got Fun*: 'the rich get rich and the poor... get poorer... get laid off... (or) get children'. The lyrics are yours to choose – in Spanish, all of them rhyme and have the ring of truth.

But things are changing. These days inequality in Latin America has dropped to its lowest level for 30 years – and this at a time when the rest of the world is seeing the gap between rich and poor grow dramatically. The business weekly *The Economist* will tell you that this has nothing to do with socialist governments – but they would say that, wouldn't they? At the same time they identify government transfers (they fail to note by progressive governments) of wealth to the poorest and support for an increase in basic public education as key factors.[3] It is notable that Venezuela under Chávez's Bolivarian policies has the most equal distribution of income on the continent. Its Gini Index rating has dropped five points to 40.99 per cent in 2008.[4] By contrast the US is becoming ever more unequal and now has a Gini rating of nearly 47 per cent. The Gini Index was invented as a measure of equality and inequality – a factor not included under other economic indicators such as gross domestic product (GDP) or per-capita gross national income (GNI).

This Latin American shift has been a long time in the works. The capitalist economic model is not popular. There is little faith that private control of the all-important resource sector will provide anything but an unbalanced economy with unimpeded benefits flowing to foreign investors, which is how it has always worked before. Throughout the 1990s, corruption continued to be a huge issue in the region, with the political classes from Mexico City to Buenos Aires exercising their sense of entitlement to public funds. Over the same period, however, political space has opened up. The disgraced military's grip on political life has loosened and the region has experienced a dramatic growth in social-movement activism in response to militant neoliberal policies. There were epic struggles over land in Brazil led by the 300,000-strong rural landless workers' movement MST. The Confederation of Indigenous Nationalities in Ecuador (CONAIE) helped to show two neoliberal presidents the door. In Bolivia, urban movements centered on El Alto (a working-class suburb of La Paz) and coca farmers organizing against the US War on Drugs set the stage for later successful struggles to overturn the privatization of gas and water. In Argentina, there was a flowering of unemployed and worker movements, following the severe economic crisis and bank collapse of 2001, that resulted in a mass popular uprising. Citizens seized control of neighborhoods and workplaces with the slogan *Que se vayan todos!* ('throw them all out!'). Argentina still has one of the most vibrant and oppositional civil societies on the continent.

A continent moves to the left

But it was in Venezuela that the impact has been the most far-reaching. The conservative political class in that country, which had hitherto squandered the nation's oil wealth, was further compromised by its complicity in the 1989 deaths of some 600 demonstrators who were gunned down in Caracas while protesting against IMF-inspired austerity measures. A decade of strife led to the 1998 election of the radical populist Hugo Chávez, whose internationalism and oil money encouraged similar movements in other countries. Soon, almost all of South America had elected governments of the Left – the only two exceptions being Colombia and Peru. Many of the leaders of these governments have come with personal histories of underground activity and prison time during the dark days of military dictatorship. Dilma Roussef of the Workers' Party, who was elected President of Brazil in 2011, is a former guerrilla and political prisoner. The austere José Mujica, elected President of Uruguay in 2010, served more than a decade in solitary confinement for resisting military rule in his country. Michelle Bachelet, the former social democratic President of Chile (2006-10), was a former political prisoner tortured and then exiled by the Pinochet dictatorship in 1974. Memories run deep. Since the original round of Left victories, only Chile and Paraguay have returned to the neoliberal fold. Unlike earlier, isolated ruptures with the Washington Consensus, this was such a sweeping continent-wide rejection that there was little that the US government could do (especially after a coup to overthrow Chávez had failed) but sit on the sidelines and snipe. By 2005, the big neoliberal plan for a Free Trade Area of the Americas was dead in the water. Instead, a Community of Latin American and Caribbean States was formed that excluded North America and marginalized the US-dominated Organization of American States.

Of course, the story is more complicated, as what some call 'Bolivarianism' and others '21st-century socialism' turns out to be a variegated and contradictory phenomenon. It has different faces in different places, ranging from fairly moderate social democracy to quite radical attempts to build a new kind of socialism from below. But even in its more moderate form, in places such as Brazil and Chile, it has shown far more resilience and refusal to fold in the face of bond-market pressure than have their center-left colleagues in Europe and elsewhere. Part of this is certainly due to a shift in public opinion on the continent in favor of rethinking the relationship to capitalism in general and the domination of the United States in particular. The boldness is underwritten also by radical movements willing to take to the streets either in defense of advance or disdain of retreat. Socialist aspiration to create an alternative to capitalism usually exists more in the *barrios* and workplaces than in the cabinet offices. It is worth noting that Chávez, when first elected, went out of his way to cloak himself in moderate respectability. He was pushed to more radical policies by the hostility of his enemies (including a failed coup in 2002) and the insistence of his popular base (tricked so often before by fine words). But Chávez himself proved an able (if somewhat egotistical) microphone for picking up and amplifying the sentiments and interests of Venezuela's dispossessed.

To grasp the complexity of the left turn in Latin America it might be useful to sketch the borders of agreement and disagreement between the different political tendencies on the Left. It seems generally agreed that there is a need for a socialism involving more than a passive electorate supporting a legislative program imposed from above. There is also a consensus, whatever sympathies exist for the Cuban revolution, that the notion of an autocratic state socialism imposing its dictates from above is a thing of the past. Cuba still holds much Latin American sympathy for the manner in which it has stood up for more than half a century to the hostility of the mighty US just 90 miles to the north. But there is also a critical determination in the new Latin American socialism about the integrity of each country's path. Cuba itself is going through interesting changes after emerging from the Soviet shadow. The jury is still out on whether such changes can evolve into a popular democracy that breaks the mold of one-party rule.

Social democracy with backbone

There is also a sense in Latin America that the Left in power needs to be something different from a warmed-over version of the Right. This form of social democracy has backbone. Beyond this, the agreements start to unravel. There is little consensus on issues such as the measures needed to preserve the environment, the extent of public ownership, or the extent to which power should be devolved from the political class and the institutions it controls.

There have been bold moves to resist privatization and US bullying over such issues as military bases and the war on drugs but, with the partial exception of Venezuela, there have been few efforts to extend public ownership by socializing private capital. In Bolivia, the government of Evo Morales has taken back control of the natural-resource sector, including water and gas, but has by and large left economic production in private hands. It is arguable that this lack of socialization of the productive sector marks the limit of 21st-century socialism – or at least the Bolivarian face of it. In Venezuela, the government has resisted any real extension of workers' self-management into the vital oil sector and has ignored agriculture to the point of seriously undermining food sovereignty – some 70 per cent of the country's food is now imported. Instead the path has been to create new institutions – public banks, a non-corporate public media, a series of pan-Latin American trade pacts and other South-South economic arrangements.

Where Left governments have generally excelled is in seriously addressing long-neglected poverty via targeted social programs. In many cases, extreme poverty has been cut in half over the past decade. There has also been strong support for the co-operative sector (in Venezuela under Chávez in particular, the number of co-ops went from around 700 to tens of thousands)[4] and for worker takeovers of mostly bankrupt or deserted businesses (particularly in Argentina, but elsewhere as well). There have been a number of direct-democracy initiatives devolving power to local community councils in Venezuela and to indigenous territories in Bolivia and Ecuador. In Brazil, the left wing of the Workers' Party pioneered the idea of a participatory budget in the southern city of Porto Alegre, building on dissatisfaction with conventional urban structures. Although this has had mixed success locally, it has become an important standard of municipal democracy on the continent and beyond. A focal point has been to move beyond granting welfare from above to local power embedded in workplaces and communities. The best political thinking within the Bolivarian movement draws from Mexico's indigenous Zapatista movement's notion of 'leading by following' or 'leading from behind'. The basic idea here is to identify those popular tendencies at the base of society that are pushing forward a radical democratic alternative and to foster and sustain them in their endeavors. So movements to take over factories and estates, to set up community-controlled health clinics or to establish popular forms of municipal governance, are encouraged rather than artificially created from above.

The basic tension within this kind of leftist movement is between those who think that their goals are best achieved through a more efficient and practical top-down politics, be they career-minded Bolivarian bureaucrats in Caracas or timid social democrats in Brasilia, and those who insist on a new kind of democratic ecosocialist politics from below. The seductive luxuries and pomp that come with national power will always be dangers, as will a tendency towards a kind of easy pragmatism that drowns dreams in practicalities. The differences express themselves over both limits and methods: popular assemblies or bureaucratic dictate; behind-the-scenes maneuvers or the politics of the street. In Bolivia, Ecuador and Argentina, there is real disagreement between the Left in the streets and that in government. The Ecuadorian government of Rafael Correa, in particular, has had some sharp disagreements with the country's Left over issues of the environment, resource development and indigenous rights. Here, as elsewhere, there is a political cost to giving in to the pressures of the corporate Right. If politics is the art of the possible, and agitation the art of the desirable, they need to be kept in creative tension without either being entirely abandoned. The large demonstrations spearheaded by activists for free public transportation that shook urban Brazil in June 2013 were further proof that the political class, whatever its Left credentials, is on notice to deliver the goods. The demonstrations were remarkable both for their spontaneity and their willingness to reject nationalist circuses and demand attention to popular needs. Who would have ever imagined a popular upsurge in football-mad Brazil that demanded funds be diverted from hosting the World Cup to meeting the housing and transport needs of the poor?

Writing about the fate of Chavismo in Venezuela (before the death of its founder), Canadian journalist Jeffery Webber makes the point that:

> 'The ultimate fate of the Venezuelan experiment will be the balance of forces within Chavismo, between those in favor of democratic revolutionary socialism from below, and those bureaucratizing the process and cementing their privileges from above.' [4]

The same could be said for all the national theaters where Latin America's 21st-century socialism is trying to find its legs. The basic point is that these are not smooth, well-oiled political machines underpinning worked-out leftist electoral projects. Instead, 21st-century socialism is something a good deal messier. It is rather a diverse and multifaceted movement from below, without which any electoral successes would lose both their way and their meaning. This is also why its gains will not be easily overturned by this or that defeat at the polls, the death of a leader or the subtle (and not-so-subtle) pressures of the predators of corporate globalization. The movement is made up of slum dwellers, students, indigenous people, squatters, workers (both in and out of employment), those who survive in the informal sector, teachers, farmers, activists, environmentalists, trade unionists and many, many others. It is not that all of these individuals and groups agree in some facile show of unity – far from it. It is that they have all found a political home where they feel comfortable and from which they can work more effectively together to fight for their rights and to bring about the changes they envision of a world beyond capitalism.

Defending and expanding the commons

Another growing source of resistance to capitalist ways of doing things in the Global South is the focus on the defense of what has come to be known as 'the global commons'. The commons is eloquently described by the radical website otherworldsarepossible.org as:

The global commons is the set of natural resources, basic services, public spaces, cultural traditions, and other essentials of life and society that are, or should be, part of a public trust to be enjoyed by all people and cherished for the planet's well-being. Another way to conceive of these assets is how it is said in Spanish: el bien común, *the common good. Behind*

> *the commons is the fundamental idea that life, information, human relationships, popular culture, and the earth's riches are sacrosanct and not for sale.*[5]

So the commons at its most basic includes the earth and all its eco-systems: the atmosphere, fresh waterways and oceans, soil, forests, and all forms of life that interact with them. We all need and have a right to have access to these in order to survive. An expanded definition would also include those things we hold in a public collective sense – public healthcare, libraries, sidewalks, bus and subway systems, public insurance, pensions, urban and wilderness parks, public broadcasting, museums, public education and so on. The definition these days is often extended also to include the products of human labor/knowledge, forming a kind of intellectual commons, including such intangibles as medical knowledge, genetic and computing codes, access to radio and TV frequencies and the freedom of digital space. This is a particularly hotly contested realm as the struggle continues between open and free access and the attempt to construct a regime of intellectual property. An extended notion of the commons raises profound questions about who 'owns' the products of the mind or even if they can legitimately be owned. Some commons are local (neighborhoods or water supply), some are regional (watersheds and forests) while others are global (oceans, biodiversity, the internet). So the commons is a comprehensive notion that includes much of the wealth of both nature and society.

Since the birth of capitalism there has been a constant pressure to transfer the ownership and control of common resources into private hands. In the earliest days of privatizing land in Britain, this process came to be known as 'enclosure' and was even then very unpopular. This has always been a word largely associated with unjust expropriation and exclusion. It is a term still applicable today as commonly held resources are taken for private profit, mostly by large corporations with the complicity of the state. Conventional economics would have it that this is the most efficient way to exploit such resources for the good of all. This view underpins the capacity of mining companies, private utility providers, international agribusiness corporations, for-profit health providers and others to take away from the commons and then sell back to the public – or at least to those sections of the public with the means to pay. Such privatizers avoid the use of the notion or language of the commons, relying instead on a 'frontier' metaphor so that they may paint themselves as bold pioneers. The implication is that this frontier is somehow 'empty' when in reality it is just commonly held in some way. The word 'privatize' has also fallen out of favor because of the negative implications of World Bank and IMF policies in the 1980s and 1990s. Privatizers now prefer to claim that they are actually in favor of something called 'public-private partnerships'. The alienation of commonwealth means a loss of control not only of services and resources themselves but also over how they are developed – and, in the case of the natural commons, this process almost always sacrifices sustainability and ecological health for speed and expediency at the lowest possible cost.

The Global South still contains large numbers of people who depend on a natural subsistence economy directly rooted in access to the commons. These include those practicing slash and burn and other forms of small-scale agriculture, inshore and offshore artisanal fishers, forest people who hunt and harvest, and nomadic peoples, many of whom are dependent on access to common grazing land. Often (but not always) such people overlap with indigenous or tribal societies. Such people can be described as living 'off the grid'. There is also a smaller but still important group of such people in the Global North. Some of these maintain this mode of existence by choice rather than being born into it. This kind of life may seem unimaginable to those living in the centers of large cities but hundreds of millions of people still live in this traditional or adopted way. Such peoples have, by their very dependence on direct access to the commons, become humanity's first line of defense in preserving its integrity. This has also become a focus of the resistance to capitalism and a spur for imagining other more democratic ways to manage the commonwealth.

Protecting water and forest

Water has become a major flashpoint in the struggle to defend the commons. In certain dryland areas this has to do with scarcity but it also involves a process of 'mining' by which a renewable resource is, through misuse and over-exploitation, turned into a non-renewable resource similar to a deposit of minerals. In the case of water this has happened in a number of ways: draining aquifers by over-use; promoting water-intensive industrial agriculture; degrading water through pollution; or disturbing natural water catchment and river systems through watershed destruction or the construction of mega-dams.

Water politics is a growing source of tension between the survival economy and industrial demand. Sometimes this arises from resistance to flooding from large dams or other water-diversion schemes – high-profile campaigns have, for example, been waged against the Sardar Sarovar Dam in the Narmada Valley in western India and the Xayaburi Dam on the Mekong River in northern Laos. Such dams are set to remove livelihoods and lands on which local smallholders and fishers in these areas depend. There are dozens of such dam fights stretching from the Amazonia region of Latin America to the remote regions of southwest China and the Yangtze River Basin above where the world's largest dam, the controversial Three Gorges, was constructed. What is at stake in these far-flung campaigns that are pitting smallholders against national bureaucracies and private construction interests is the integrity of the world's great river systems. Although many of these resistance movements have not succeeded, they have gradually built a constituency of eco-opposition that has inspired a national search for alternatives.

The rural poor have also been in the forefront of protecting forests and watersheds. Among the pioneers here were such figures as the murdered Brazilian activist Chico Mendes, who fought for the integrity of an Amazon Basin besieged by ranchers and timber companies, the feminist-inspired Chipko tree-hugger villagers in the foothills of the Himalayas, and the late Kenyan activist and Nobel Peace Prize winner Wangari Maathai, who helped found that country's Green Belt movement. Such brave pioneers not only brought these issues into prominence but also showed the world that ecological health was an issue that spread far beyond Western middle-class activists.

Such struggles are no longer isolated but have exploded on a number of fronts, and there is a growing awareness on the part of at least some planners of the importance of watershed integrity. There has also been movement at the UN, with equal water access recognized as an international right and the birth of an Alternative World Water Forum to battle against privatization. According to the United Nations Development Programme: '(The) water crisis is largely of our own making. It has resulted not from the natural limitations of the water supply or lack of financing and appropriate technologies, even though these are important factors, but rather from profound failures in water government.'[6]

There have been legislative victories such as India's Forest Rights Act and political victories such as the successful battle against water privatization in Cochabamba, Bolivia. New flashpoints of struggle have emerged, among them the misuse of water by the Coca-Cola company in India, the destruction of watershed forests to produce biofuels for export, and the pollution of water sources by international mining companies from Guatemala to Indonesia. There have also been successful referendum initiatives to declare water as a human right and against the privatization of water in Uruguay and Italy.

Another area of urgent concern for commons activists is the recent growth in large private landholdings in poor countries in the Global South. It is smallholder agriculture that is most immediately affected by the huge land grabs that started at the turn of this century and picked up speed with the crisis in food supply and prices that occurred in 2008-9. Since then, between 80 and 200 million hectares of land in the Global South have been gobbled up by transnational corporations or sovereign funds controlled by national governments.[7] These are land grabs on a scale not seen since colonial times. The purpose of these investments vary. Some are initiated by 'food insecure' nations such as China, Japan, South Korea and the oil-rich Gulf States. But most such major land grabs are still carried out by private corporations so as to take land out of food production and instead grow export crops – this might mean cultivating flowers for the European market or lucrative biofuels to help maintain Western transport systems based on the private automobile. Here the motivation is usually gaining a lucrative return and the players behind the scenes are a variety of investment, pension and hedge funds. Such land grabs often result in the expulsion of small farmers and the loss of food sovereignty for poor countries with populations vulnerable to hunger and malnutrition. Pakistan, Cambodia and Sudan are particularly egregious targets in this regard.

The idea of defending the integrity of the commons is no longer limited to those living in the survival economy but now involves those who are more removed from it but still dependent on its bounty for their survival. In theory this is all of us. But for those for whom electrical and water bills consume an infinitesimal part of their personal budgets, this may not be a serious issue – or at least not a financial one. But for urban dwellers (often squatters) living in slum communities – now about one in six people on earth – the privatization of land and utilities means the expropriation of a commons on which they depend for their survival. With neoliberal privatization, the idea that utilities are public goods that should be provided at minimal cost to all has pretty much fallen out of favor. Instead, corporations have developed private industries that are more committed to their shareholders and executives than to service recipients. Where they are allowed, they gobble up essential goods (electricity, water, sanitation services) and repackage them for sale at a profit.

This is another frontline in the defense of the commons. From places like Soweto and other massive townships of the poor in South Africa to the cities of the Bolivian Andes like Cochabamba and El Alto, direct-action groups have been rising up in defense of the idea of public utilities as common goods. After just two years, the Tanzanian government managed to escape from a privatized contract with the British company Biwater, which had reportedly cherry-picked middle-class areas of Dar es Salaam and ignored the poor – Biwater sued for breach of contract but lost. Elsewhere, in countries such as Côte d'Ivoire, Senegal and the Philippines where water services have been privatized, prices have shot up, making water unaffordable for poor households. Remunicipalization of water and sanitation services is also occurring in such large urban areas as Paris and Buenos Aires as well as medium-sized ones such as the Canadian city of Hamilton, Ontario.[8]

The high water mark for privatization maneuvers was the 1990s. It is now, however, undergoing a resurgence because the private-sector economic crisis has spilled over into an underfunded public sector stretched by bank bailouts and economic pump priming. A good example of a large-scale privatization is in El Salvador where the public power company CEL was restructured and partially privatized in 1998 which resulted in the layoff of 52 per cent of the workforce. Privatizations in port and airport facilities have had similar results. El Salvador's unions face a new multi-pronged privatization law called P3 which threatens 'public-private partnerships' in everything from municipal services to higher education.[9] Similar fights are going on in almost every corner of the globe.

While struggles over particular aspects of the commons have become everyday events, what is still missing is a more comprehensive sense of the commons as a whole that needs protection and extension. Such a commons must include the upstream (watersheds, national parks, fisheries, local food production systems, sustainable forests) as well as the downstream (public goods and services such as water, electricity, sanitation and communications). This commons could and should be governed by a system of democratic checks and balances that ensures ecological health as well as sustainable livelihoods for people at both ends of the stream. This would be the best way to resist the blandishments of market fundamentalism.

The commons as a fount of hope

The commons is not just a battlefield between corporate predators and those who resist them – it is also a source of hope for those willing to imagine a world beyond capitalism. It represents a space between the private market and the political state in which humanity can control and democratically root our common wealth. Both the market and the state have proved inadequate for this purpose. In different ways, they have both led to a centralization of power and decision-making. Both private monopolies and state bureaucracies have proved incapable of maintaining the ecological health of the commons or managing the fair and equitable distribution of its benefits.

The conservative ecologist Garrett Hardin's belief that the commons is facing a tragedy was based on the notion that individual self-interest in exploiting common resources was undercutting the overall health of those limited resources.[10] Hardin maintained that individual self-interest trumps any more thoughtful notion of preserving resources for future use. External restraints needed to be imposed. To prove his point, Hardin used the example of the individual herder taking more than their share of pastureland. It assumes a human behavior that is all too familiar to those who have seen the global fishery depleted and seen watersheds destroyed by those hungry for land to grow crops. Hardin's solution was to divide up the commons into private property and public goods administered through the market and the state. But it scarcely seems to follow that if the commons is turned into private property or put under the supervision of some distant state bureaucracy that it will fare much better. These days, the two will likely form a 'public-private partnership' and any regime of fair-use regulation will go out the window. There is also a question of scale. Is it better to have many small inshore artisanal fishers or to turn the fishery over to Big Capital and the high-tech trawler fleets? How could it make sense to push small farmers off food-producing land so that large biofuel producers can help keep our unsustainable love affair with the private automobile alive? When Hardin's self-interested human nature is combined with large-scale private ownership, it is likely to yield ever more short-sighted results. It is no way to manage the commons.

It is far better to rethink how the commons is managed and to include as many of the players as possible so as to achieve a better result. If decisions rested with local communities or regions, in combination with users of various types both local and remote (environmentalists, fishers, miners, farmers, consumers), and were placed within a legal framework that takes future generations into account, it would seem likely to produce a more durable form of stewardship. This might also in the long run develop other potentialities of human behavior than the narrow self-interest that Hardin so feared.

An alternative to capitalism must in the end be based on a more complex sense of the human than orthodox economists' notion that we are all hardwired to a rational calculus of individual costs and benefits. The influential commons theorist Elinor Ostrom proposes a different, more optimistic, notion of the human potential for managing the commons. Ostrom won the Nobel Prize in economics for her seminal 1990 work

Governing the Commons.[11] She believes that: 'we live in a web of social relations infused with norms and values; we are intrinsically co-operative and as a result collective action is possible and may lead to sustainable and equitable governance practices.'[12] Ostrom does not commit herself to an ambitious political program of replacing state and market with more direct democratic practices. But she opens up the debate about how the commons should be governed rather than just assuming the market abetted by the state can handle the job. For Ostrom, a process of 'deliberative democracy' is essential if there is to be proper human stewardship of the commons. Others in the commons movement carry the analysis further and see in the commons the potential to restructure the underlying configuration of power between markets, states and societies.

Democratic promise

This begins to give some indication of the democratic promise of the commons as a potential cornerstone in working out an alternative to capitalism. It takes on the ascendant neoliberalism of the commons privatizers while avoiding the dysfunctional effects of top-down state planning and centralized public ownership that have undercut previous efforts to build a socialism centered on the state. It moves beyond the sterile debate between an inadequate state and a rapacious market. Instead it explores the idea of a decentralized eco-democracy founded on what in the commons is vital to both human and biosphere survival. It extends democratic decision-making to ensure egalitarian economic outcomes. Here is one example of a commons-based popular initiative from Greece (made vulnerable to privatization pressure because of the debt crisis):

> *'In the Greek city of Thessaloniki, a coalition of citizens' groups called Initiative 136 is creating a new organization to compete with Suez [a French water corporation] in the tender for the*

acquisition of the shares and the management of Thessaloniki's Water and Sewerage Company. The dual goal is to prevent privatization and replace the model of state administration that has failed to protect the public character of water resources and infrastructure, and secure genuine democratic control of the city's water by its citizens. The management would be organized through local co-operatives, with citizen participation. Initiative 136 is an effort to pre-empt privatization before it is implemented, with an attractive concrete alternative in the form of improved public management.'[13]

Multiply such initiatives many times and root them in the plethora of different struggles currently being waged over the commons and you start to get a sense of radical democratic promise. While the term 'commons' has many meanings, both spiritual and philosophical, it is explored here mainly as a political project. The core strategy is to design institutional arrangements that move beyond state and market and put the commons back into the service of society as a whole. The underlying principles of such institutions need to be based on a variety of forms of self-organization and collective ownership rights, which is exactly what Initiative 136 in Thessaloniki is attempting to achieve. There are many other examples. The fishers of the Turkish port of Alanya manage their part of the global commons by allocating each fishing boat a clearly prescribed area of the Mediterranean according to the results of a lottery. They then rotate from area to area: from September to January, every day, each boat moves east to the next location. From February to May they move west. All fishers get the same opportunity as the fish stocks migrate. The system is collectively monitored and enforced. Problems are rare – and generally resolved in the local coffee house. As Ostrom notes, 'Alanya provides an example of a self-governed, common-property arrangement in which rules have been devised and modified by the participants themselves and also are monitored and enforced by them.'[14] The co-operative self-management of a particular commons is likely to pay more attention to its long-term health and viability. The implications can be far-reaching.:

> '...the abiding logic of the commons is not based, as we have seen, on a balancing act between the roles of the state and the market, but on the idea of a polycentrism, decentralization and agreement between those touched by common problems. More co-operation, less competition. More conservation and the dynamics of resilience with regard to resources and their relationship with the environment than erosion, limitless exploitation and unstoppable appropriation.'[15]

Other commons-based movements, striving for an alternative ethos, are just getting started. Attempts to create a horizontal commons democracy include the Right to the City movement and other urban initiatives inspired by the French libertarian Marxist Henri Lefebvre. Right to the City has gained traction in South Africa with the Abahlali baseMjondolo shackdwellers' movement, which is active in a number of cities across the country, and in the German city of Hamburg, where it has inspired a network of squatters, tenants and artists. It has become a rallying point also in US cities such as Miami and Boston, and a source of inspiration in India, where Rajapalaya Lake in central Bangalore has been the focus of a fight to maintain a livable urban commons in very crowded conditions.

Some struggles combine resistance and vision. In Quebec, 2012 witnessed a remarkable movement of students against the commodification of education, which put the besieged notion of free advanced education back on the public agenda. Their struggle, which helped to bring down a provincial government, could act as a template for those trying to recover the educational commons from the pressures of commercialization. In the 1990s there was a successful national fishers' strike in India that prevented the government of the time from handing over the Indian fishery to big trawler operators. Countless other examples, big and small, dot the daily press but are often just restricted to obscure websites.

Commons battles tend to gain attention when they precipitate or are part of some larger struggle that involves active confrontation with those in power. This is, however, really just the tip of the iceberg. If you examine the specialist literature you will discover that almost everywhere there are attempts to make the self-management of the commons a reality. There is an *International Journal of the Commons* which acts as a forum for debate about commons issues and case studies of successes and failures. A quick look through the table of contents provides a sense of both the scope of the commons and of initiatives being taken to extend their democratic self-management. Here are but a few of the examples:

- The commons in a multi-level world
- The European Union Baltic fishery
- Irrigation systems in southeastern Spain
- A new marine commons off the Chilean coast
- The cockles fishery in coastal Ecuador
- Commons resource management in southern Namibia
- Technology-dependent commons
- Participative action in Kafue Flats in Zambia
- An environmental response to the globalizing forestry industry
- Southeast Asia: rewarding the upland poor for saving the commons
- Self-governance of the global microbial commons
- Icelandic health records
- The commons and community development in the eastern Caribbean.[16]

This list provides evidence that the commons is not some obscure issue but one that runs in one way or another through the lives of most of the world's people, often on a daily basis. The scope is truly impressive. It also has a lot of complex nuts and bolts to it with which we need to get to grips. But it is a complexity we need to embrace, eschewing simple-minded monocultural solutions in the process. This is an ongoing effort that will involve many.

But it must remain beyond the scope of this book. Here we are just emphasizing the peril and potential of the commons. It has the potential to become a new legal basis for the foundation of common rights to set against the threat of public-private partnerships. If this does not succeed, then we risk everything, not least our genetic make-up and that of the plants and animals with which we share the earth, being turned into corporate private property. The stakes are high. The commons are connected to our sense of place, to our identities, livelihoods and self-expression – ultimately even to our survival as a species. This is a good place to start envisioning a radical democratic alternative that gives people a fundamental say in their individual and collective futures. As such, recasting our relationship with the commons should take pride of place as we build an alternative to capitalism.

1 nin.tl/HE8CaV **2** Eduardo Galeano, *The Open Veins of Latin America*, Monthly Review Press, New York, 1973. **3** 'Gini back in the bottle', *The Economist*, 13 Oct 2012. **4** Jeffery R Webber, 'Venezuela Under Chávez', in *21st Century Socialism*, Fernwood Books, Halifax, 2011. **5** 'Defending the Global Commons', Other Worlds, nin.tl/1b3HjPP **6** Focus on the Global South, nin.tl/HE9kVI **7** grain.org **8** nin.tl/1b3HURG **9** nin.tl/HE9yMy **10** Garrett Hardin, 'The tragedy of the commons', *Science* 162 (1968). **11** Elinor Ostrom, *Governing the Commons*, Cambridge University Press, 1991. **12** Danijela Dolenec, 'The commons as a radical democratic project', br.boell.org Nov 2012. **13** municipalservicesproject.org **14** p2pfoundation.net/Cybernetics_of_the_Commons **15** Joan Subirats, 'The commons beyond state and market', opendemocracy.org 12 Jul 2012. **16** thecommonsjournal.org

8

The democratic emergency

Politics has been professionalized and depoliticized. One party seems pretty much like another – with the result that voters' distrust of politicians has soared and participation in elections has tumbled to new lows. Occasional eruptions of protest are not enough: something needs to change.

'Today, anxiety is a first principle of social life, and the Right knows how to exploit it. Capital foments the insecurity that impels people to submit to its demands.'

Ellen Willis

The burst of capitalist triumphalism that met the implosion of orthodox communism at the end of the 1980s did not last long. There was no New World Order or abrupt halt to class politics drowned by some euphoric end of history. On the other hand, there was no peace dividend of the kind we had a right to expect as a result of ending the Cold War military stand-off. The neoliberal back-patting and self-congratulation quickly gave way to new embarrassments and new enemies. The assault on the Islamic world and the staunch defense of all things Israeli resulted in blowback from political Islam of all stripes that remains ongoing. The deregulatory climate that was supposed to free up capital to deliver jobs and prosperity turned out to be a speculative shell game, as finance capital proved willing to sacrifice almost anything for high executive compensation and lavish bonuses. Hundreds of thousands have lost their jobs and houses on both sides of the Atlantic as a result of the 2008 financial crash.

But despite the crisis and mass moral revulsion that followed the crash, coherent opposition in the heartland of European and North American capitalism has so far failed to emerge. There have been flare-ups of disgust, such as the US-inspired Occupy movement, or the more substantial resistance to the austerity model that governments around the Mediterranean rim are trying to impose on their most vulnerable citizens. But only really in Greece has there been deep, system-wide opposition together with proposed alternatives to the neoliberal rescue of the irresponsible rich at the cost of pretty much everyone else. A more common pattern is a kind of anti-politics, exemplified by the Five-Star Movement in Italy led by the comic Beppo Grillo or by widespread street resistance (Spain's Indignados movement, for example) from the disaffected all over southern Europe. Such protests, while completely understandable, have had meager results – and have allowed the national security state to resort to ever more authoritarian forms of rule.

The protests are symptomatic of a malaise affecting both the Left and the citizenry as a whole. 'I'm mad and I'm not going to take it any more' is more moral revulsion than thought-out politics. Showing disdain for the political class may make good theater but does little to rally a majority around the possibility of substantive change. It leaves the field of 'responsible' opposition to a Center-Left that has already capitulated far too much to entertain creative alternative ways of reorganizing society. Activism is also absorbed into non-governmental organizations;

these organize around single issues but their politics are restricted by government charity laws and a misplaced ideology of professionalism. As a consequence, as we saw in the last chapter, movements for significant radical alternatives largely come to life these days in the Global South rather than in the increasingly beleaguered welfare states of the North.

One problem with the anti-politics of protest is that it can move in almost any direction. In the US, it gave birth to the crazed Tea Party movement, and in Europe it has contributed to the modest rebirth of the fascist Right. It tends towards scapegoating (immigrants, crime, users of public services, trade unions) rather than thoughtful alternatives. It can rally around charismatic figures who are thrown up by the moment but as quickly disappear or else give in to personal ambition and are absorbed into the political class. Once the enthusiasms of the moment start to fade, a demobilizing apathy begins to set in. Private satisfactions and old addictions take hold again. The point is that conventional politics is being monopolized by a corps of professional politicians who are both too compromised and lack the radical imagination to go against the momentum of the market. It is essential to move beyond a revolt against politics and to do so we need proposals that break the monopoly on public life and empower society to start reshaping itself – rather than counting on our unrepresentative representatives to do it for us. Otherwise we are left with a sad neoliberal fate poignantly described by the Miami activist Tom Crumpacker:

> 'The neoliberal political system, which poses as democracy but in fact is the system of oligarchy and empire, is now referred to as the "end of history" for political thinking. Clearly this characterization is accurate. Political thinking on the neoliberal line has reached a dead end. Commodity society, where structural political progress has become impossible, has no future but disintegration. The culture of individualism has separated us from each other, binding us together not by our

values but by enmeshing us in a net of commercial relations. Our mass consumer society has become an overpowering depoliticizing force.'[1]

Rolling back the Sixties

Depoliticized and merely symbolic revolt must be seen against the background of a long-term decline in political awareness and engagement that dates back in most places to at least the insurgent challenges of the 1960s. Whether in Beijing, Prague, Paris or San Francisco, this was an era of broad challenge to the existing structures of both corporate capitalism and bureaucratic communism. Elites across the globe took fright. Social movements made significant gains, with the expansion of the welfare state, greater regulation of corporate abuse and an opening up of the public sphere. Workers were on the offensive, with gains both in real wages and in benefits. Ultimately, though, most of these Sixties movements failed to achieve their more radical aims of a deeper, more egalitarian and participatory democracy. In the end, the generation of 1960s radicals even failed to defend their limited progress towards creating a more socially responsible capitalism.

But the alarm among élites and their intellectual acolytes was palpable. In many cases it involved police and even tanks. But it also involved a kind of marketization and privatization of political thought. The late Samuel Huntington and the Trilateral Commission were in a sense typical of a whole coterie of counter-insurgency intellectuals and academics who ran to the aid of frightened power and privilege. They were quick to tell them what they wanted to hear. There was a Crisis in Democracy (the name of their now infamous 1973 Trilateral Commission Report) and it was destabilizing the kind of orderly progress that the élites so cherished.[2] Things had got out of hand. People's expectations were more than could be tolerated. They didn't understand democracy and the need for limits. Unions and other 'special interests' were just too demanding. Everyone was too concerned with their rights rather than their responsibilities. Democracy needed discipline rather than excessive license. Their vision of democracy was one of limited representation accompanied by disciplined obedience between elections. While most Sixties activists held that the problem with democracy was that there wasn't enough of it, these counter-insurgency intellectuals held that there was just too much.

While the radicals had their ambitious ideals, the counter-insurgency intellectuals had the ear of power. With a few exceptions, they also had a compliant corporate media that acted as an effective loudspeaker for the business oligarchy. Disruption and idealism were off the menu. Obedience and normalization were the order of the day. By the 1980s, a sweeping offensive in favor of deregulation and privatization was well under way, led by Margaret Thatcher in the UK and Ronald Reagan in the US. All of a sudden 'entitlement' became a kind of official swearword and 'incentive' the gold standard. Old 19th-century notions of the undeserving poor came back into vogue, as did the long-discredited, dubious doctrine of 'trickle-down economics'. If only capital could be freed from the fetters of over-taxation and meddling bureaucracy, we could return to the golden days of perfect competition (which have never actually existed). This program was called 'neoliberalism' as it harked back to the days of the original market economists who believed that, left alone, the market would provide a system of perfect competition that would ensure fair treatment for all. When the communist world imploded that was just the icing on the cake for capitalist triumphalism. There was no alternative. Any notion of the collective good was buried in the shopping malls and online boutiques. Wages stalled but credit boomed. A kind of galloping inequality took hold and has never looked back since. In the US the top one per cent of income earners had 10 per cent of the income in 1980 but by 2007 they were at 23 per cent and climbing.[3] Other major corporate-controlled economies show similar gaps. It all seemed to work, just as long as people could meet their mortgage and credit card payments, and states could maintain deficit finance. But that couldn't and didn't last.

A hollowed-out democracy

Democracy in its original Greek sense meant self-rule by a designated population of citizens – admittedly excluding, in the case of Greek city-states, women and slaves. Throughout history the degree of self-rule and inclusion in the franchise has ebbed and flowed. Much blood was shed over expanding the right to vote to include men without property, women and racial and other minorities. Today, most accepted definitions give all citizens over a certain age the right to vote. But what they are voting for is becoming pretty murky. Self-rule is certainly not on the agenda. Electoral politics is, by and large, held to work best with a multi-party system allowing voters a choice. But a choice of what?

Since the neoliberal counter-revolution of the 1980s there has been a hollowing out of democracy to the point that large portions of the electorate no longer bother to cast their ballots. The political parties around which the system is organized are supposed to represent different philosophical and policy options. Since the 1980s (and arguably before) the major parties of left and right have converged in most of their basic political assumptions. These days, rather than dividing over substantive policy issues, they compete over questions of style and personality. The decisive factors in winning an election are access to the funds (provided in many cases by corporate capital) needed to buy media time, and expertise at manipulating the electorate. Ideological convergence is not just a question of careerism and ambition – although the desire to rise within the political class is certainly a factor. But since the neoliberal assault of the 1980s, globalized capital has had virtual veto power over even mildly progressive economic justice measures.

By the time Reagan and the Thatcher Conservatives had left the field, their center-left replacements – the Clinton Democrats and Tony Blair's New Labour – had also shifted dramatically in a conservative, pro-market direction. Means-testing welfare, further privatizations and maintaining business confidence were more important for them than any program that shifted significant resources in a serious attempt to tackle inequality. Clinton and Blair represented the capitulation to a neoliberal consensus that has taken hold of the major parties in most multi-party systems. What has emerged is a kind of managerial state with only minor shades of difference between the political parties aiming to run it. This consensus means that most issues of substance are fudged and shelved. The last serious attempt to alter the balance of forces in a major Northern industrial country was the first term of the François Mitterrand's Socialist government in early 1980s France. It was subjected to intense pressure from global capital and money markets and soon backed away from its ambitious program of extending public ownership into the financial sector.

It is odd that, during the Cold War, it was the accusation of a totalitarian lack of choice that the West hurled at the managerial party-states of the communist East. Now a different but still quite anti-democratic managerial politics is squeezing what little choice remains in multi-party systems. The means is not so much direct repression (although that always lurks in the background) as the encouragement of a demobilizing apathy best summed up by the well-worn phrase 'they are all the same'. The public is encouraged to think only as taxpayers concerned with getting 'value for money'. The more generous bonds of citizenship, empathy and solidarity are dissolved in the acid of possessive individualism. Any idea of the common good is lost. In the process, several positions on the political spectrum have virtually disappeared as significant factors – these include political liberalism and traditional conservatism, which have both been marginalized by economic neoliberalism in combination with authoritarian national security doctrine. Edmund Burke's idea of a conservatism that actually 'conserves' things (be they traditional values, communities, old buildings, or the environment) would be unrecognizable to most people who think of themselves as conservatives today. Similarly, political liberalism – the belief in fairness and human rights – has been subsumed by the expediencies of power, whether the party involved still describes itself as liberal or not.

Expectations of representative rule are effectively discouraged. This can be seen in the shrinking numbers of voters who bother to show up at the polls. The US is notorious for low turnouts, arguably because it offers the least choice, between the tweedledum Republicans and tweedledee Democrats. Between them there is much heat and name-calling but few significant policy differences. The massive military budget and meager public provision go unchallenged. For non-presidential congressional elections, turnouts are below 50 per cent. But virtually every European country has also seen fairly steady declines in voter participation rates since World War Two. Turnouts for elections to the European Parliament are even lower than for national elections.[4] The extremely undemocratic architecture of the European Union is at least partially to blame here. If whatever democracy there is exists at the level of nation-states, while vital issues are being decided on a Europe-wide basis by unaccountable technocrats, isn't that a design for retreat from political engagement?

All of this comes at a time of serious economic crisis that has cost many people their dwellings and livelihoods, and polls show a discontent bordering on fury with the incumbents who are attempting to impose a draconian austerity regime almost everywhere. There has also been a decline in the membership of political parties, as such parties become centralized political machines relying on well-paid consultants, pollsters and other professional staff rather than on volunteers. This can be very clearly seen in the drop in membership of the parties of center-left social democracy – the British Labour Party dropped from over a million members in the 1950s to just 200,000 by 2006, the German SPD by a third from 1990 to 2005 and the Swedish Social Democrats from a million in 1990 to just 152,000 13 years later.[5] This centralization of power reduces the say (and enthusiasm) of party members in setting policy direction. Even elected party representatives tend to be marginalized in favor of an inner circle of professional manipulators that shields the executive branch from too much popular pressure.

Complacency and crisis

The depoliticized culture has been tightly engineered by the political class, the vast majority of whom believe that all the big issues have been settled. They are complacent that a liberal system of limited political representation and a globalized market economy are here for the foreseeable future. We live, they seem to believe, in the best of all possible worlds. Imagination has been foreclosed. As the Red Queen told Alice in Lewis Carroll's *Through the Looking Glass*, 'when I use a word, it means just what I choose it to mean, neither more nor less'. Policy is reduced to the degree of tinkering one should engage in so as to achieve a healthy economy and a secure state and society. Security is the newest word in the Red Queen's vocabulary. After all, one cannot be too secure. But security for some is, of course, insecurity for others. Political issues today focus around how best to cater to the rich and the corporations in the hope that they might 'invest' some of their ill-gotten fortunes to provide us with elusive employment. From the 'general public' below there is mostly cynicism and apathy – with the occasional outburst of street anger.

There lurks behind the scenes a half-formed awareness that something is dreadfully wrong – although what it is and what to do about it remain elusive. Bob Dylan caught the sensibility way back when with his lyric 'there is something happening here but you don't know what it is, do you, Mr Jones'. As noted earlier, our species faces an ecological crisis, the consequences of which are proving increasingly dire. In addition, the social terrain on which industrial society was constructed – stable well-paid employment won through hard trade union struggles; a safety net that caught the most vulnerable and gave people a realistic hope that their children would be better off than themselves – is now a thing of the past. Precarious employment is now the order of the day. In Canada's largest urban conglomeration of Toronto/Hamilton, a recent report concluded that barely half of the workforce had full-time jobs that included benefits. The rest worked in part-time and/or underpaid jobs, the number of which had increased by 50 per cent over the previous 20 years.[6] The tendency towards this kind of precarious work is very gendered and racialized, with women, immigrants, minorities and, increasingly, young workers forced into such employment. A similar tendency with a great deal of regional variation can be identified right across the industrial world. This is related to a number of other trends, such as the rise of service employment, the destruction of workers' rights through labor 'flexibilization' laws and the shift of industrial employment, mostly to Asia.

Service workers make up nearly 80 per cent of the work force in the UK and the percentage is even higher in the US.[7] Most such jobs are insecure, unorganized and comparatively poorly paid. There has even been a phrase coined to describe those (often young) workers who are in precarious employment. They are 'the precariate' – to distinguish them from the once-stable proletariat. China now has more than twice as many industrial workers as all the original G7 industrial countries combined. Although this has meant a dramatic improvement in the lives of many Chinese, it has also led to some of the most exploitative labor conditions in the world. China has now become the most unequal country in Asia, with a Gini Index rating that has moved from 0.21 in the 1960s to 0.46 today.[8] Chinese workers are not taking this lying down, with widespread protest and industrial action despite the constant threat of repression by the communist party-state. Galloping inequality might be considered the proudest achievement of international neoliberalism.

The consequences of this are dire for working people the world over – and increasingly also for those who think of themselves as middle class. Large numbers are falling through the cracks and finding that the social safety net has been yanked away by the neoliberal Right, often with the compliance of their center-left 'opponents'. The implications for those who would craft an alternative to capitalism are dramatic. The goal of an 'industrial socialism' propelled forward by the struggle of industrial workers is no longer on the table. What is needed now is to craft a new ecosocialist democracy – but this is a hard hill to climb in a society that is profoundly depoliticized and has an atrophied sense of possibility. But the very instabilities built into the system can be counted upon to generate constant tensions. As the wily German playwright Bertolt Brecht pointed out: 'Because things are the way they are, things will not stay the way they are.' The comfort zone of our political class will need to be breached if anything significant is to change. The political failures on everything from climate degradation through excessive military spending to control of the speculative banking industry speak volumes. Radical problems call for radical solutions.

1 'The politics of depoliticization', Tom Crumpacker, *State of Nature*, Winter, 2006, stateofnature.org **2** Michel J Crozier, Samuel P Huntington, Joji Watanuki, 'The Crisis of Democracy', Trilateral Commission, nin.tl/1arB6uC **3** inequality.org **4** For detailed studies of voter turnout, see the work done by the Swedish International Institute for Democracy and Electoral Assistance, www.idea.int **5** Dylan Riley, 'Bernstein's Heirs', *New Left Review*, Jul/Aug 2012. **6** Laurie Monsebraaten, 'Half of GTA and Hamilton workers in precarious jobs', *Toronto Star*, 23 Feb 2013. **7** Andrew Smith, 'On Shopworking', *New Left Review*, Nov/Dec 2012. **8** Göran Therborn, 'A New Class Landscape', *New Left Review*, Nov/Dec 2012.

9

The autonomous rupture

The Left has cut itself adrift from its old obsessions and is embracing new thinking. On the theoretical side, the ideas of the 'autonomists' have made an important contribution. But theory is not enough – and new alternatives may be more likely to emerge from the practice of making our communities and workplaces more democratic.

'*The very thing that makes you rich, makes me poor.*'
Sidney W Bailey (sung by Ry Cooder)

There has over the past four or five decades been a dramatic shift in perspective on the part of the Left that still harbors serious intentions of replacing capitalism with a more humane social system. This position on the political spectrum up until the 1960s was monopolized by a very conventional Marxism that combined an economic determinist class analysis (with its sad base/superstructure metaphors) with a belief in a vanguard party that would lead the proletariat to victory. This was supposed to be a scientific certainty. Certainly this orthodoxy has had its heretics and renegades quick to point out its authoritarian proclivities and ultimately its similarities – exploitative growth based on the subordination of wage labor – to the very capitalism it claimed to oppose. By the 1960s the Marxist-Leninist paradigm had begun to lose its luster for many radicals and by the 1990s, with the collapse of the Soviet Union and China's embrace of capitalism, the game was pretty much up. It still hangs on in places like North Korea or among Trotskyist and Maoist groupuscules held together by a nostalgia for people's wars and the storming of winter palaces. Where such movements have gained serious political traction – as in Nepal, where the Maoist-inspired UCPN(M) has widespread support – they have abandoned hardline Leninism to embrace more heterodox thinking and give support to ethnic and sexual minorities. They have transformed themselves through the process of political struggle into something closer to the Bolivarian Left of Latin America.

What emerged first out of the New Left of the 1960s and then out of the anti-globalization movements of the late 1990s was something quite different. There was a good deal of variety but some common themes can be observed. The new model of activism is based on the notion that popular struggles need to be defined by the activities of workers and their allies rather than by the command structures of professional revolutionaries. The language of the 1960s New Left was remarkably different from that of the Leninist old guard. It had a kind of populist flair that tended at times towards the outrageous – 'be realistic, demand everything', 'participatory democracy', 'obsolete communism – the leftwing alternative', and of course 'all power to the people'. The May 1968 revolt in France added the poetry of the French Situationists, as in 'all power to the imagination'. The emphasis had definitely shifted away from Bolshevik command politics in favor of creating alternatives from below. In the anti-globalization movement, the language evolved further: 'One No, Many Yeses' was borrowed from the radical indigenous Zapatista movement in southern Mexico, while there were various plays on the notion of globalization, as with 'Globalize resistance' or 'Globalization from below'.

In the early 21st century we had truly arrived at a different time and a different culture with a 'movement of movements' coming together to share experiences and perspectives at World Social Forums on almost every continent. Here were the culture jammers, net activists, anti-sweatshop groups, debt-relief committees, fair-trade advocates, homeless and landless organizations, those who would remake the texture of urban life or those who organized around gender and sexual preference, indigenous and ethnic groupings and a plethora of others. This was all a long way from the iron discipline of the Comintern and one could almost sympathize with the old leftists scratching their heads nervously at the bewildering polycentrism of it all. These days there is also a tone of desperation creeping in, born of the combination of ecological meltdown with austerity regimes imposed to pay for the speculative extravagances of the wealthy. As the new slogan goes, 'There is no planet B'.

These tendencies have much more in common with the libertarian notion of socialism than the state socialist tradition. Still, many of the historical issues that divided the Left are still in play: the practical versus the idealistic, the horizontal against the vertical, compromise or confrontation. Plus, Lenin's old question (if not his answer) still hangs in the air: 'What is to be done?' In analytical terms, it is perhaps most useful to focus on the self-description of many of these groupings as 'autonomous'. The word comes from the Greek and means basically self-determination. It has its roots both in the anarchist tradition and in that of dissident Marxism dating back at least to Rosa Luxemburg. There are parallel strains of development coming from various schools of anarchist thought but also touching a reading of Marx that has never died out completely. Important thinkers in this regard include the workers' council movement of the World War One era, the Caribbean activist scholar CLR James and those close to him, Cornelius Castoriadis and the

1950s French grouping Socialisme ou Barbarie, though there are many others too numerous to acknowledge.[1] All of these claim the direct inheritance of a libertarian Marx (for them the real Marx) who never stopped championing the autonomous right of working people to overcome their exploitation and remake the world. There has, of course, long been a battle over Marx and what he actually stood for. For the autonomists, the real Marx is the one of the *Civil Wars in France* who championed the direct democracy elements of the Paris Commune and famously wrote: 'the working class cannot simply lay hold of the ready-made state machinery, and wield it for its own purposes'.[2] The autonomists' reading of this and other of Marx's writings boils down to the idea that a 'socialist state' is actually a contradiction in terms. This brings them into closer proximity to the traditions of libertarian thought that are associated more with anarchism than with classical Marxism.

The identification as an 'autonomist' is now widely spread if variously and sometimes poorly understood. Autonomists are determined not to surrender their freedom of thought and action to the agendas of others, be they parties, states or the corporate world. Today, the identification as 'autonomous' stretches from the confrontational anarchist Black Bloc (now spreading beyond the industrial North to Egypt) to those who would set up alternative communities and institutions in the cracks of capitalism. It is the main current in the popular upsurges that have surfaced first as the anti-globalization and then Occupy Wall Street movements in the US and now the anti-austerity movement that is sweeping southern Europe. It is bound together by two basic tenets: first, a kind of militant refusal of politics as currently practiced in favor of a horizontal agency for achieving revolutionary change; second, a belief that such an agency prefigures new non-hierarchical social relations that can be the basis for a world beyond predator capitalism. Many autonomists see themselves as closer to anarchism than Marxism and speak of an 'anarchist turn'. But the theorists and thinkers of the movement still draw heavily from a libertarian reading of Marx.

The Italian influence

Modern autonomism really found its legs as a peculiarly Italian expression of the 1960s New Left. It was a movement much more rooted in working-class revolt (particularly that of young workers) than New Lefts elsewhere that tended to have a more diverse youth base. It proved to be one of the more stubbornly resilient of the New Lefts, producing an impressive range of organizational forms and theoretical innovations. It was vital in Italy's hot autumn of 1969 and in upsurges throughout the 1970s that won major concessions from a fearful corporate élite. Like its fellow movements elsewhere, it vacillated between experimentation with new organizational forms and falling back onto old 'vanguard party' formulas that eventually proved the undoing of the movement in Italy and beyond. In the Italian case, the 1977 rise of the Red Brigades and their terrorist misadventures gave the state security apparatus the excuse it was looking for to defame and ultimately smash the movement as a whole. But, surprisingly, much of the thinking that shaped the Italian movement has survived and has gone on to have a broader influence on the ideas and perspectives of the current extra-parliamentary Left. Such thinkers and strategists as Mario Tronti, Sergio Bologna, Silvia Federici (of Wages for Housework fame) and most enduringly Antonio Negri were part of an intellectual enterprise that sought what they termed 'a Marxism beyond Marx'.[3] They felt 'everything must be reinvented' and so they went at it. Notions of the socialized worker and the social factory freed the worker from the old industrial plant and its deformations of scientific management and trading freedom for wages. The new regime of capital, the autonomists believed, was attempting to extend factory discipline into society as a whole – but this was also providing new sources of opposition to its rule.

These autonomists saw things coming down the road that few others on the Left did at the time: deindustrialization, structural unemployment, globalization, just-in-time production, out-sourcing, the rise of a §new technical working class and the spread of precarious employment as capital restructured itself. These days such phenomena are simply taken as commonplace. But the Italian autonomists' most startling innovation of all was that they saw capital's restructuring strategies not simply as an assault on workers' lives and livelihoods but also as an opportunity to shift the ground to a more profound stage of liberation.

From an autonomist point of view, the destabilizing of the workforce and the extension of factory discipline into society as a whole – seen today in the national security state and a highly policed welfare system – allows for a more fundamental opposition to the exclusive power exercised through executive sovereignty. Openings for self-management, popular assemblies and a variety of forms of direct democracy provide a potential rupture with the system of command. The new instabilities in the precarious world of work are also seen by autonomists as another source of potential liberation as the grip of work discipline is loosened on the 'multitude' – Negri's term to replace the stricter Marxist notion of proletariat. They reject the full employment fantasies of traditional socialism and see a potential for an assault on the wage labor relationship that Marx identified as so basic to capitalism.

From an autonomist perspective, this is the path to creating a democratic form of production controlled by neither state nor private property but by workers themselves. Negri in particular, in his recent writings, sees the technical worker as an important catalyst in this process. In the view of Negri and a number of other radical thinkers dealing with the 'information society', the form of post-Fordist intelligent labor who design and run computer networks and other knowledge-based industries are having their imaginations blunted and their freedom curtailed by Silicon Capital.[4] Negri is in this sense loyal to the technological optimism of Marxism in believing that this modern breed of intelligent 'socialized' worker, created through modern production, can be the cutting edge of a new horizontal communism. But some of this is also clearly an exaggeration as most jobs in this postmodern economy are not glamorous thought-work but belong to security guards, data-entry clerks, shopworkers, janitors, fast-food workers and those at the low end of the service and 'caring' industries looking after the young, old and infirm.[5] What, if any, are the bonds of solidarity between such workers and élite computer programmers and others holding highly prized jobs in the various fields of technological design? On this question the autonomists are largely silent.

Autonomists on the future

Autonomist radicalism infuses much of the Left's most creative radical political writing these days. It has seeped from continental Europe into the Anglo-Saxon world in the writings of John Holloway (*Changing the World Without Taking Power* and *Crack Capitalism*), Andy Merriweather (*Magical Marxism*) and Harry Cleaver (*Reading Capital Politically*). But it has probably reached its highest point in the sometimes brilliant trilogy of Negri and his US collaborator Michael Hardt, which is in a sense the most coherent attempt to move Marx beyond Marxism. This ambitious, impressive work (*Empire*, *Multitude* and, most recently, *Commonwealth*) outlines new innovations in the way capital exercises power and teases out the opportunities, both actual and potential, for mounting an effective challenge. These autonomists often disagree with each other but on one thing they seem to be of common mind – the need for a strategy of exit from capitalism. They believe that it is not enough to take over the existing institutions – the state, jobs, weapons, factories, technologies – and turn them in a different liberatory direction. Instead they place their hope in a radical 'exit' from the system after which 'everything must be reinvented'. In doing this they ask questions that subvert not only capitalism but much of the classical socialist tradition as well. What is the purpose of a democracy of limited or symbolic representation that is so far from the actual exercise of popular self-rule? Why participate in an economics of centralized growth that spreads inequality while destroying the biosphere? What would be the purpose of any self-management if workers continued to produce the same weapons and waste? If we use the coercive techniques of the enemy to destroy their power, won't we end up by in effect becoming them? For the autonomists, hope lies in the refusal both of work and other forms of participation dictated by capital's system of command from above. This insistence on taking a viewpoint outside capital and its demands is a major contribution to providing a new radical starting-point as we mount a challenge to our commodified world.

The autonomist perspective tends at times, however, to be quite vague and abstract on many points, especially what society beyond capitalism will look like and the way in which political opposition to capital is to gather itself and co-ordinate a decisive shift of the balance in its favor. The autonomists would perhaps counter that they are playing a long game, identifying tendencies that in the end will be vital in undermining the system. On questions of the exact shape of the future, the autonomists adhere to the traditional Marxist prejudice against utopian speculation. The closest they come to a programmatic perspective is this:

> 'The program outlined by Negri and his comrades includes: guaranteed equalitarian incomes; the reconstruction of a participatory civil society outside the state; the building of networks of localized, user-run social services; radical innovation and rearrangement of the working day; and the passage of production into communal, co-operative forms, some of which they see foreshadowed in feminist organizational experiments.'[6]

But this raises as many questions as it answers. How can we have 'guaranteed equalitarian incomes' without some political institution to do the redirecting of social wealth and to co-ordinate and guarantee such incomes? The general tendency is for the autonomists to see a new society emerging out of a decentralized counter-culture that has been created by those exiting from an increasingly dysfunctional capitalism that is no longer able to satisfy the expanding needs of the population. The exit is part of the necessary rupture – breaking from a life of wage labor in the service of wasteful production to something saner. The exit will also, however, involve escape from a state system that is less and less democratic and more and more dependent on its coercive police functions to maintain gross inequalities of wealth and power.

But exit isn't enough. After we are out the door, then what? The notion of a void of poetic dreams (a kind of 'butterfly life', as Andy Merriweather would have it in his *Magical Marxism*) will not be very reassuring to fellow citizens deformed by the constant insecurities of capitalist existence. If we expect others to take the leap to freedom with us we need a coherent and practical sense of what this freedom will look like on the other side of the door. Otherwise we risk the fate of previous counter-cultures – well meaning but marginal in their appeal. Easily isolated and swallowed up by the momentum of the system. Or brutally suppressed while uncomprehending majorities stand by and shake their heads. As the radical critic Stanley Aronowitz puts it:

'How can a new series of social arrangements transform the state from an institution of hierarchical repression and control into a series of agencies of co-ordination of a series of self-managed cooperative enterprises that organize the production and distribution of material goods and the dissemination of knowledge and information – in which case the state is no longer the state but something else?'[7]

Co-operative alternatives

The autonomists need to overcome their distaste for debating the possible shape of a post-capitalist future and how we might build a bridge to it. But their emphasis on the seeds of that future lying in the present remains a fruitful antidote to the neoliberal mantra that 'there is no alternative'. Every day, all over the world, people are working to create alternatives: there is, for example, a vast co-operative economy made up of production and consumer co-ops, worker co-operatives, credit unions, co-operative poolings of capital, co-housing schemes that involve hundreds of millions of people. Some are very large, such as the dense network of Mondragon co-ops in the Spanish Basque country, while others are tiny urban neighborhood or village ventures that vary widely in strength and resilience. There are self-care co-operatives such as the Cooperative Home Care Associates in the Bronx borough of New York City, which has 800 low-income owner-members (mostly poor women of color) who tend the home-bound elderly, poor and disabled.[8] In some places these co-operatives are a large and important player in national economies. Take the Italian co-operative movement. This has 16,000 producer co-operatives, while, with five million members, Italy's consumer co-ops are second only to those of Japan, accounting for 60 per cent of the country's home and healthcare system. Their track record has also been good.

> Over the last 20 years, at a time when the Italian corporate sector was cutting its workforce, the largest of Italy's co-ops were growing in size and reach and outpacing their competitors in the number of jobs they created and in market share. Moreover, in the retail sector, the co-op system has sustained nearly 15-per-cent growth while keeping retail prices five per cent lower than most supermarkets, and two to three per cent lower than those of their fiercest competitors.[9]

These co-operatives are in turn rooted in a broader social economy made up of NGOs, self-help groups, trade unions, voluntary associations (often with unpaid leadership), all engaged in not-for-profit activities. In the Canadian province of Quebec, this large and growing 'third sector' exists between the public and the private, including *caisses populaires* (credit unions) and solidarity and worker-shareholder co-operatives. In Canada as a whole, this social sector is estimated to provide a livelihood for almost as many people as those employed in the beleaguered Canadian industrial sector. Add to this the vast informal sector where most people in the Global South (and increasing numbers in the North as well) are forced to strive for a living in various marginal self-help enterprises, and you quickly come to the realization that employment provided through corporate largesse is a shrinking sector of the global economy.

This is not to say that this social economy is in opposition to capitalism – in fact it often plays a kind of damage-control role, ameliorating some of the social fallout resulting from the neoliberal shredding of the safety net. The point is that millions of people are choosing to work in alternative fields where reciprocal values beyond the ethos of individual self-advancement are what counts and where there is at least the possibility of more democratic input than that dictated by traditional capitalist command. The value of reciprocity is key here, both in the present and as the basis of a post-capitalist future.

> *'Reciprocity is the social mechanism that makes associational life possible. It is the foundation of social life and of social capital – the predisposition of people in a society to work together around mutual goals. In its elements, reciprocity is a system of voluntary exchange between individuals based on the understanding that the giving of a favor by an individual will in future be reciprocated either to the giver or to someone else.'*[9]

For the militant autonomist and the radical Left more generally, this is all pretty tame reformist stuff. They point out quite correctly that careerism, bureaucracy and narrow self-interest have far too often derailed co-operatives and civil society. Its democratic commitments remain imperfect and its values are easily eroded by participation in the unregulated market. Its ethos is tainted by an individualism that erodes solidarity. It can become a self-serving enclave of privileged workers who exclude newcomers.

But why should we have any more faith that the autonomous movement's notion of an oppositional counter-culture of independent production and reproduction is going to be that much different? As long as the values and momentum of capital are dominant in society and remain unchallenged in a fundamental and effective way, it seems unlikely that alternatives, no matter how noble, will be able to do much to shift the balance. If there is no decisive challenge to the logic of capitalism, such alternatives will continue to be marginalized and deformed – and, if they are too overtly anti-capitalist, possibly suppressed outright. The November 2008 attack of the French state on a small anarcho-autonomist community in the Corrèze region of central France is not atypical. Without the widespread belief that capitalism needs replacing and the attraction of a credible alternative, the political Right (and its dancing partner the Center-Left) will continue to play on people's deeply embedded insecurities about the economic future and will continue to popularize notions of 'sound fiscal management' that play out as endless rounds of austerity and growing inequality. The Left needs a political presence that establishes both the necessity and viability of a better future – and some sense of how we might get there.

Only if this starts happening will we be able to stop preaching to the choir and reach out to those who live in the suburbs, populate the shopping malls, hold down two or three low-paid jobs to feed their kids, and see no way out of the spiritual desert that capitalism is quickly becoming. To create an ecological democracy means to reinstate active citizenship as the centerpiece of political life that can draw hundreds of millions of people (and probably billions) into shaping what an alternative way of living might look like. If such large numbers are to buy in, there needs to be a convincing notion of how things could be different. The autonomy movement's exit strategy is a first step but will remain marginal without the popularizing of such a vision.

Politics and anti-politics

These days it is pretty easy to become alienated from the hypocritical doings of the political class almost everywhere. Large numbers of people have retreated into a kind of 'passive-aggressive' political apathy in which intimate life and the pleasures of spectacular consumption and addiction are the only things that make life worth living. The political Right has been far more successful than the Center-Left at mobilizing this hostile apathy, with cheap appeals to self-righteous anger in their pseudo-campaigns to 'roll back the state' – an anti-politics in the service of politicians.

The Left that is still committed to radically challenging capitalism has tended to gravitate towards a different kind of 'anti-politics'. One form of this might be termed the 'autonomist moment'. At worst, this translates into a kind of serviceable if unambitious negation – 'whatever they are for, we are against'. Where it moves beyond negation it is preoccupied with not having its activities captured by the existing structures of the system. It thus eschews participation in the dominant system of production as well as the arena of conventional politics. This can lead to a kind of in-group élitism that is by implication, and sometimes quite explicitly, disdainful of those who have not yet managed their own 'exit' from the system. Like conventional theoretical Marxism, it has a specialized language and speaks to itself rather than a broader constituency.

It is much easier to figure out what the autonomous movement is against than what it is for. In their provocative trilogy, Hardt and Negri are frustratingly vague on what they see as a potential future and how to get there. Not for them the pedestrian political program or utopian speculation as to how things might end up. On questions of organization, they fall back on cyber-vagueness:

> *...coalitions, rainbows, rhizomes, networks, and webs [which have been salient features] of anti-capitalist movements in the last decade, for Negri, denote the search for a politics adequate to 'the specific form of existence of the socialized worker,' in which the new is not something unitary, but something manifold. The paradigm is not solitary, but polyvalent. The productive nucleus of the antagonism consists in multiplicity.[10]*

What? It would be hard to convince any but the most committed (or those with the least to lose) to risk their futures on such a throw of the dice. To gather the popular will to challenge a powerfully embedded capitalism, much more defined political and economic alternatives need to be on the table. Flashmobs and spontaneous happenings have their place but, without more of an institutional core to offer a rooted base for consistent opposition, I fear marginalization will continue to lurk.

This is not an argument for the return of some magical and all-knowing revolutionary party to lead us out of the wilderness. Those days are gone and good riddance. An adequate political vehicle needs to be multi-centered and multi-layered to cope with challenge on many fronts. It should include political parties of varying orientations with a more grassroots democratic caste who might contest elections but who need to refuse power in most situations. There are already a few examples of such fledgling parties such as Québec Solidaire or the 28 parties associated with the European Left in the EU. There needs to be a coming together of political representatives in popular organizations (radical caucuses, student groups, committed unionists, workers and unemployed centers, women's organizations, anti-racist activists, tenants and homeless movements, NGOs, environmental groupings and many other forms of resistance) who are accountable to more than just themselves as individuals. Such assemblies and their political outgrowths need to create a political pole in society that consistently makes a practical case for an alternative set of proposals over decades. It needs to be established in the public mind (whether one is in agreement with it or not) that this is a coherent alternative to the present course of corporate growth and ecocide.

One of the problems social movements face is the difficulty they have in thinking strategically. Their spontaneous comings together allow for tactical reflection on immediate issues: Where should we march? How should we deal with the police? What is our main message? They are, however, poorly equipped to think strategically. How do we position ourselves over the next five years? Where is the most productive use of our resources? How do we explain ourselves to a dispirited and disillusioned populace? How can we outflank this new austerity offensive? How do we convince people that this new pipeline project or that super-highway will just lead us further down the road to eco-collapse? Social movements tend to be reactive to the provocations of capital and the state and outraged by their celebrations of their own power (hence the resistance at the meetings of the G8, World Bank/IMF and the World Economic Forum at Davos). This leaves little space for actually taking the initiative to focus on popularizing alternative proposals for how life might be lived or how to turn the finance sector into a democratic public service or how society's wealth might be distributed in new ways.

The most effective and coherent protests against the austerity offensive in southern Europe took place in Greece, where the political party Syriza has been able to make common cause with the autonomist 'movement of the squares' that was spearheading street opposition. This is a fragile alliance that has had to overcome the autonomists' distrust of verticalist parties manipulating them for opportunistic purposes. But the effect of both levels of opposition working in tandem is that the anti-austerity message has dug much more deeply into Greek political culture than elsewhere.[11] In the murky world of Italian politics, the case is not so clear. The Five-Star Movement, led by the comic Beppe Grillo, has all the attributes of an expression of anti-political disgust. It is certainly not about putting forward a coherent alternative to replace capitalism with an egalitarian eco-democracy. But its success at the polls and its refusal to broker a deal for a small slice of power have struck a chord with Italians tired of the 'same old, same old' from right to left. The Party's core principles (the five stars) are fairly vague and minimalist: publicly owned water, better transport, development, internet access and environmentalism. But the very fact that Grillo's anti-politics could catapult *Movimento 5 Stelle* overnight from nowhere into the leading vote-getter in the country speaks to the desperation of Italians searching for something radically different.

The challenge is how to move beyond the anti-politics of autonomy and populist anti-heroes like Grillo to a reinvention of politics as a liberatory political space – to base a politics on post-capitalist principle rather than self-serving expediency. This will not be possible without some kind of well-thought-out and coherent program that speaks to growing discontent and rallies it in a radical direction. People need to know what you are for rather than just what you are against.

What do we do about the state?

Part of the difficulties to work through lie in the different attitudes towards the state. There is every reason to rethink the coercive state as it is currently constructed. It is a block to any notion of democracy in its most profound communal and socialist sense: the self-rule of the polity. The problem is that an understandable anti-statism both serves many masters and limits the political possibilities of real resistance to a minimalist anti-politics. It has become political sport to denigrate the political class. And no-one does it better than politicians themselves. The whole neoliberal appeal of 'rolling back the state' is a hypocritical sleight of hand used to sell market ideology. In the mean time the state only continues to expand as a coercive apparatus safeguarding corporate control and disciplining an alienated and unruly populace. The anti-politics of the opposition taps the same root as it rallies resistance. But in embracing the reflexive anti-statist anger of the streets, it leaves the political arena of imagining and advocating a different future.

In both conventional left and right readings, the state is seen as an 'instrument' to enforce arbitrary rule. Such a view unites neoliberal, Leninist and most anarchist perspectives. But the state is more than that. It is also a terrain to be fought over, using strategies that will either restrict it to its coercive functions (the conservative position) or extend its legitimizing 'welfare state' functions (the center-left line). This often takes the form of a struggle over the priorities outlined each year in a government's national budget.[12] But there is potential for a third position in this battle. This would champion the state's egalitarian obligations to respond to popular needs instead of simply catering to corporate market power, but would at the same time seek to extend the notion of democracy and embed it in communities and workplaces. Some of this is happening in the uneven developments of Bolivarian popular democracy in Latin America. It is also a position that echoes the earlier British New Left notion of being both 'in and against' the state. The hope is to ignite and foster the capacity of society to take over the 'beneficial' things the state is charged with doing in a somewhat half-hearted and often corrupt manner. It would mean democratizing the power and resources currently monopolized by the state.

This democratization could take a number of forms, as in the earlier discussion of non-statist ways of managing the commons. It could give more weight and responsibility to the social economy and to relationships based on reciprocity rather than profit. It needs to be embedded by an extensive program of direct democracy, including workplace self-management, so as to shape an economic policy favoring democratic co-operation over private monopolies. It should be possible to recall politicians and hold referenda on important issues, enabling policy initiatives from below, a constitutional decentralization of power and a far greater role for local self-governance by communities. But how to guarantee all the content of this extended self-governance would move in a humane, ecological and socialist direction? There simply are no such guarantees in a truly democratic polity – but measures like these would allow for much greater possibilities than are currently allowed with the state exclusively monopolizing power.

To embrace such a strategy, the Left needs to rethink the goal that is still cherished by many of a violent overthrow or 'smashing' of the state. This has become a dangerous and self-defeating fantasy. The days of storming the Bastille and the Winter Palace are things of the past. In modern societies where groups have engaged in terrorist assaults on the state – the Red Brigades in Italy, the Red Army Faction in Germany and a score of others, the results have been disastrous. not only for themselves but also because they provided the excuse for repression of a broader radical movement. The clandestine culture in which such groups exist tends to shape them into small authoritarian cults. Militaristic thinking quickly dominates any sense of the political. If a struggle deteriorates into a civil war, as sometimes happens with the failed states of the Global South in places like Syria and Libya, the chances of a healthy political outcome are slim to none.

The modern state has invested heavily in a sophisticated police and intelligence apparatus that has shown itself willing to go to extreme lengths to defend state interests. It will, if threatened, kill, torture, and imprison hundreds of thousands if necessary. If one state in the state system appears to be in danger others will prop it up by invasion if necessary. The case of Syria, where the regime lost all legitimacy and most popular support, shows how the coercive apparatus can hold on for long periods through the simple application of bloody terror. Today, even the most 'civilized' of states are developing cutting-edge crowd-control technologies, including microwave energy blasters, blinding laser beams, chemical agents and deafening sonic-boom machines. Then there is the 'invisible pain ray', a non-lethal 'active denial system' to control local space through crowd dispersal by applying what the US Air Force calls the 'goodbye effect'.[13] You can be sure that there are many police officers eager to test out these new toys.

Surveillance systems and techniques to disrupt clandestine groups have also reached new levels of sophistication, especially since the war on political Islam in the post-9/11 period. The urban landscape is saturated with closed-circuit security surveillance cameras and police have an arsenal of legal powers that override fundamental civil liberties. Then there is the Predator drone program for territorial surveillance and, if necessary, elimination of suspected terrorists without any due legal process. Many of these techniques have been pioneered and tested by the Israeli military and police in monitoring and controlling all resistance to their illegal occupation of Palestine. Despite this, the Palestinians continue to resist and to provide inspiration for us all. But where they have been most effective is through open organization of active nonviolence. The first and second *intifadas* were far more successful in shifting the ground and escalating the costs of the occupation than the terror tactics and suicide bombs once used by Hamas and the Palestine Liberation Organization.

The metaphor of occupation is a useful one when considering the relationship between state and society. For in many ways the state, which is supposed to represent and care for society, actually occupies it as a coercive and alien power. To extend the metaphor, the left political opposition needs to use the tactics of *intifada* as part of a broader political project that can effectively challenge the legitimacy of a state dedicated foremost to the interests and property of the privileged. But tactics need careful consideration. They need to fit into overall strategies and not expose the movement to avoidable repression and political damage. It is in this context that the question of violence (and its most recent manifestation in Black Bloc tactics for confronting property and the police) needs to be considered and judged. If the battle on the terrain of the state is to deepen democracy, autonomy of action needs to be leavened by a sense of collective purpose.

1 A good summary can be found in Richard Gombin, *The Radical Tradition,* Methuen, 1979. **2** nin.tl/17eWl8i **3** An excellent and sympathetic survey of Italian autonomism can be found in *The Philosophy of Tony Negri, Vols 1 and 2,* edited by Timothy Murphy and Abdul-Karim Mustapha, Pluto, 2005. **4** Mackenzie Werk, *The Hacker's Manifesto*, Harvard University Press, 2004. **5** For a critical appreciation of the autonomists, see Nick Dyer-Witheford nin.tl/HLhta2 **6** See Christian Garland, *The Anti-politics of Autonomy*, nin.tl/17eXnB0 **7** Stanley Aronowitz, *Left Turn: forging a new political future*, Paradigm, Boulder, 2006. **8** chcany.org **9** John Restakis, 'Tax Justice and the Civil Economy', in *The Great Revenue Robbery*, edited by Richard Swift, Between The Lines, Toronto, 2013. **10** Nick Dyer-Witheford, op cit. **11** Interview with Marina Prentoulis, links.org.au/node/3145 **12** For a brilliant discussion of the state budget as political terrain, see James O'Connor, *The Fiscal Crisis of the State*, Transaction Publishers, New York, 2001. **13** nin.tl/HLilvi

10

What should we stand for?

We need to move beyond anti-politics and have the
courage to envision and advocate for an alternative.
One such path involves embracing degrowth not just
as an ecological necessity but as a path to greater
quality (and equality) of life, putting financial capital at
the service of people, and providing a universal basic
income. We must dare to dream.

*Vision without action is a daydream. Action without vision is a
nightmare.*

Japanese proverb

The meteoric (but short-lived) Occupy movement that spread
across the US and beyond in the autumn of 2011 prided itself
not only on its radical democratic nature (termed horizontalism)
but also on its refusal to make demands. The idea here was
that to make demands was to grant legitimacy to power that
was illegitimate – and was not anyway in a position to bring
speculative capitalism to an end even if it so desired. The
movement's suspicion of the political establishment was based

on the history of previous social movements that had been lied to or co-opted with half-measures. Making demands, it was felt, would take power away from the grassroots and put it in the hands of untrustworthy and manipulable power-holders with a history of deceit and compromise.

These days, social movements can be divided into two groups. The first group rallies around specific demands – the end to a war, defense of endangered social rights, reduction in CO_2 emissions, stopping this pipeline or that mining mega-project. The other form of social movement (which some would label postmodern) is that influenced by autonomy and anarchism, which manifests itself in the places and gatherings of corporate power and its political administrators. Its adherents are sometimes unkindly referred to as political 'deadheads' (a reference to the ardent fans who used to follow the 1960s rock group The Grateful Dead). They wander from Wall Street to Davos to corporate annual meetings – wherever the élite meets – to express their outrage.

This is a politics not of demand but of 'bearing witness' to the powerful and their crimes, and showing 'you aren't fooling anybody'. Tactically, it takes on all the various hues of street politics, running from peaceful demonstration through civil disobedience to doing active battle with property and police. As previously noted, this is, in a sense, a form of anti-politics propelled by disillusion and disdain over how conventional politics is conducted in the late capitalist era. This intransigence both defines its uncompromising stance and sets limits on its appeal and effectiveness. When all opposition is thought of in terms of negation, it limits the ability of anti-capitalism to think beyond capitalist terms. This is the trap of anti-politics. Ironically, it allows the very system that is being negated to continue to set the terms of the dance: 'we promise jobs... you are lying and we don't want your jobs anyhow... how are you going to survive, then?' The rule of capital continues to frame the debate.

A third option beyond 'making demands' and 'bearing witness' is a politics built around proposing an alternative to the insecurity, compulsory labor and consumerist malaise that keep the growth treadmill in motion. 'Proposing' moves into the territory of creating a different kind of politics rather than simply reacting within the existing political arrangements or demonstrating against them. This is a departure from the habitual and safe politics of negation that characterizes so much left activity. It is risky to put forward an alternative that allows your opponents to pick out your shortcomings and contradictions or simply to dismiss you with derisive laughter. Then there is always that lurking fear of co-optation by a system that at times seems to have the absorptive capacity of a super sponge. Famously, the US muckraker Upton Sinclair exposed the Chicago meat-packing industry in his novel *The Jungle* as part of a campaign to create a socialist America. Instead he ended up with a bureaucratic and inadequate Food and Drug Administration. The eight-hour-day, once thought to be a wildly utopian socialist demand, ended up as a matter for factory inspectors. Then, of course, there is the difficulty of amplifying alternative proposals to a public immured by reactionary conventional wisdoms and tedious 'common sense' – especially in a context where radical proposals are discouraged and stereotyped by the consensus media.

Ultimately, however, there is no real choice but to put forward a set of ideas that could lead to a more appealing future for humankind within a sustainable ecological framework that gives us a chance of collective survival. Otherwise our protests become gratuitous or simply nihilistic. We are painted into a corner as dreamers and nay-sayers out of touch with the concerns and interests of ordinary folk. This is not entirely an unfair accusation. Radicals sometimes live in their own subcultural bubble and, while maintaining great faith in 'the people' as an abstraction, are quick to negative judgment of actual human beings whom they feel are tainted by consumerism and bourgeois prejudices.

We can get too caught up in the finer points of identity politics or the intricacies of inter-imperialist rivalry to bother with those folks worried about their children's homework or searching for sales at the local mall. 'Proposing' also raises the difficulties of reaching agreement (what the old Left used to call 'the basis of unity'). It is far easier to find agreement on what one is against than on what one is for. But while details can be worked out in practice, it is essential to sketch the broad outlines of a more desirable world if we are to have any chance of transcending the capitalist way of life.

If we do not have a politics and a program that speaks to the issues and problems of everyday life, we leave ourselves badly exposed. The tactics of mainstream politicians and their media to isolate and belittle social protest as disruptive and purely negative is all too familiar (and far too successful). If we are to create a rupture in the circular logic that 'there is no alternative', we need to propose one that gives people the hope that their lives could and should be better than the insecurity and tedious hardship engendered by the current speculative regime of 'creative destruction'. It is surely right to believe that fundamental change can only come through the self-activity of large numbers of people rather than being handed down from above by some political savior. On the other hand, those people need to be convinced that such change is possible and also to agree at least on the rough shape of a possible future society if self-activity is to be more than a marginal subculture.

A program for change

There is great potential for change in the cracks and ruptures of the present system and in the capacity of citizens without 'political experience' to recreate life. What follows is but one idea of how this could work. It is in no sense intended to be some kind of 'final word' but a modest starting-point suggesting where we need to go and how we might get there.

Degrowth

The idea of degrowth is a multi-dimensional concept that has to do not only with downscaling to reduce GDP but also with providing an escape from the domination of the economy. It seeks to promote social equity and recreate democracy on a more meaningful, decentralized scale.

This basic idea for the future is based on the truism that infinite growth is an impossibility in a finite world. This is the taproot of all radical environmentalism. It is pretty clear to all who are willing to take an honest look that we are running up against the limits of growth in everything from fresh water and fertile soil to the provision for employing human labor in a meaningful way within the current market context. Increasingly, we are put in the position of having to 'survive progress'. What was supposed to bring us prosperity and well-being is making life on earth more and more insecure.

This 'security deficit' is spreading from the economic underpinnings of daily life to the entire ecological framework that sustains us. The growth machine still provides unheard-of wealth for those at the top but less and less for even those people who think of themselves as 'middle class'. The busts in the boom-and-bust cycle of capitalism are becoming longer and affecting ever more people, while the booms are shorter and their benefits are generally accruing to a narrow layer of the corporate super-rich. These people also make out pretty well even during the busts that clear the economic playing field for their profit-making. In this distressing context, governments of both the Center-Right and the Center-Left have to one degree or another embraced a set of austerity proposals designed to curtail public/state activities in a desperate attempt to restart the growth machine.

As we have shown elsewhere, this not only may not be possible but it almost certainly is not a good idea. What we need is to escape from an economy that produces instability and inequality, and is unsustainable both in the quantity of goods it produces and in the energy-intensive and polluting ways that it produces them. So any left alternative needs to face this dilemma squarely. The best way to do this is commit to a policy framework of degrowth. Not long ago this would have been denounced as a program of Malthusian trickery on the Left – an attempt to keep the poor in misery. But while growth has drawn the poor out of the countryside of the Global South, it has not pulled them from their shanty towns or protected them from dangerous and demeaning factory work. From the factory collapses in Bangladesh through the mass suicides of beleaguered farmers in India to the plight of Chinese factory workers in Pearl River Delta factories like that of the huge Foxconn complex, this growth needs to be counted in victims rather than simply celebrated in GDP statistics. It is true that, in India and China and a few other places, economic growth has created a burgeoning wealth and a middle class of millions that would have been unimaginable 50 years ago. But, as the middle classes of southern Europe can readily attest, this prosperity is paper thin and could be easily washed away by the bursting of the next speculative bubble.

The degrowth movement is in its infancy, born amongst the rubble of growth on the Mediterranean fringe of Europe. It is less than a decade old but has already produced an intellectual and experiential rupture from the current limited categories of Left and Right. Its roots are, however, much older and can be found in many of the traditions already explored in these pages, from indigenous radicalism to libertarian socialism. Advocates of degrowth (*décroissance* in its French original) believe in 'having less to live better'. As one degrowth activist points out:

> '*This not only means a reduction in consumption, production and resource use, it also calls for a fundamental rethinking and restructuring of our coexistence and a move toward a society characterized by autonomy, frugality and solidarity. The movement is gaining followers in the crisis-shaken countries of*

southern Europe. The people there are questioning a system that has not kept its promise of prosperity, and are experimenting with alternative forms of economic and social organization.[1]

So what would a degrowth policy framework look like? For one thing it can never be thought of as strictly an economic policy. Economic thinking and decision-making has for too long been the strict preserve of economists who claimed to understand the mysteries of the market and of bankers and other corporate power-holders who manipulate these markets for their own ends. Degrowth is very much a program of economic democratization based on the belief that material growth needs to be replaced with an economy of sufficiency. It contends that economic decisions should be taken in the public sphere by those most directly affected by them: by workers and local communities, and as part of a democratically derived notion of the public interest. The underlying principle is that unlimited economic growth is neither sustainable nor viable because its activities cause the earth's ecological limits to be exceeded. For reasons of both contemporary and intergenerational equity, economic degrowth is necessary. Some of the basic principles that underpin degrowth are listed below.

- Emphasizing the quality of life as measured in convivial culture and human relationships rather than the quantity of life as measured in consumer goods.
- Prioritizing the local in everything: in decision-making, in energy and agricultural systems, in the disposal/reuse/recycling of waste, and so on. The aim would be to achieve as high a level of community self-sufficiency as is reasonably possible.
- Downshifting – a term used to describe a reduction of the ecological footprint of both individuals and communities.
- Reducing working hours to eliminate ecologically and socially damaging work and implementing a social wage or

guaranteed income to support an expansion of community-defined volunteer opportunities.

- Allocating resources democratically so that degrowth would take place on a just basis – replacing the current practice of dealing with economic crisis and shortage through austerity policies that unfairly affect the less well off who are more dependent on public provision.
- Reducing dramatically unecological forms of living such as suburban sprawl and encouraging a more equal distribution of population between rural and urban areas – but with enough density in urban planning to avoid waste in providing services.
- Revitalizing political life through decentralization and direct democracy, involving popular assemblies, workplace democracy and referenda – as well as citizen juries to maximize participation and discourage the emergence of a professional political class.
- Lessening profit-seeking and speculative economic activity at the expense of the Global South.

Obviously such an extensive program has many implications for both public policy and everyday life. It would mean something entirely different for a resource-poor African village than it would for High Street Europe. A transition to such a society would be complicated and would involve many trade-offs and reforms but also militant commitment to the final goal of a convivial degrowth. Some of the basic principles, such as fairness, self-sufficiency and local democracy, could in different ways be applied everywhere. To bring about such a transition, there would need to be dramatic changes in a number of areas, including global trade (a lot less of it), taxation (geared to achieve a radical redistribution of wealth) and the taxing of the 'material flow through' involved in resource extraction and most manufacturing (so as to limit these areas of growth to an ecologically survivable level). But I will briefly explore here two areas that are particularly vital to the transition: finance and the wage-labor system.

Bringing finance under control

The task of how to manage economic calculation effectively is vital to building any kind of alternative. How do we co-ordinate a complex economy that interacts across the world and has highly evolved divisions of labor? How can the equilibrium of what and how much to produce, and at what price, be resolved? Some of this will be made more straightforward by a degrowth that privileges local economies and sustainable levels of production. Still, it remains a vexing issue. The socialist goal of holding productive resources in common often stumbles at this point. State control of the economy through orthodox communist top-down planning proved difficult to sustain, especially as state socialist economies evolved in complexity and in the needs of their populations. Chronic shortages and poor-quality goods are not something the Left can simply shrug off. Anarchist 'participation' paradigms (such as Michael Albert and Robin Hahnel's Parecon) seem hopelessly mired in endless meetings and cumbersome co-ordination procedures. All the same, we need to put forward a credible alternative that will establish democratic control of capital flows so as both to slow their growth momentum and to redirect them towards socially useful investment. A good place to start is with what is euphemistically called 'the financial-services industry'.

The socializing of capital markets is essential if we are to ensure that people control capital rather than the other way around. We desperately need to be able to redirect finance (capital and stock markets controlled through private banks and their satellite institutions) away from paper speculation and investment in harmful production and towards alternative projects of sustainability that would support democratic degrowth. As noted earlier, many multiples of the world's material wealth are currently held in paper bets (futures and derivative markets are the worst) that have an inbuilt dynamic not only towards unsustainable growth but also towards destabilizing lives. Almost everyone is affected, from small farmers in the Global South who produce coffee, bananas or other export crops to those who cling to precarious employment and mortgages in the Global North. The paper wealth in this casino economy is one of the main reasons for the exploding inequality that is tearing at the fabric of almost every society in the world. Furthermore, the financial-services industry uses the public sector as a cash cow. This goes way beyond billion-dollar bailouts of the 'too big to fail' gambling addicts and includes such business-as-usual matters as public banking insurance and a capital bond market that regularly siphons off billions of dollars in tax resources. The Bank of England in 2009 estimated this subsidy to private banking in the UK alone to have a yearly value of $107 billion – more than the total spent on education and social security.[2]

A way must be found to take these decisions around what, where and how much to invest away from private industry and put them into the public sphere. This could be done in a variety of ways such as through regulation, taxation and various policy supports for social investment. Yet the 'too-big-to-fail' banking industry has proved it has the resources and can hire the skills (accountants, lobbyists, propagandists) to avoid such controls. Look at the way the world's big banks turned their own failures in the 2008 banking crisis into the sovereign debt crisis of 2010. This is an old game – 'privatize profits and socialize costs', a kind of socialism for the rich. Ultimately these decisions need to be taken away from private industry entirely and made on a democratic political basis that includes criteria other than profitability.

The financial-services industry has had a long and illustrious history that has seen its image shift from the staid conservative banker to the hip money-manager making (and losing) billions at the tap of a computer key. The current financial *nomenklatura* congratulate themselves on their creative acumen, which has resulted in record profits and losses in a paper economy that has less and less to do with where and how most people live. Stock values and profit rates may ebb and flow but the one thing that never seems to shrink is the financial compensation awarded to CEOs and the trader class that surrounds them. Whether through record compensation levels, stock options or the golden handshake upon departure, these folks make out like bandits amidst the evictions, job losses and disappearing pensions.

The instabilities associated with the operators of the financial-services industry are many and various, but the fundamental point is that they are more interested in paper speculation and bankrolling consumption than in the mundane tasks associated with lending for productive purposes. They have been granted a lending capacity that is far in excess of their holdings, and this can cause a liquidity crisis if things go south – which at some point they usually do. Public authority has allowed banks to usurp the *de facto* creation of money (through unsustainable expansion of credit), which dilutes the public power to control the money supply. The major private financial institutions across the globe have become highly centralized into a kind oligopoly that has a stranglehold on the world's financial system. This became worse after the 2008 financial crisis when those that failed were eaten up by those that had not. That has put the financial-services industry in an even more powerful position to resist regulation and sensible tax reforms – such as the entirely sensible and long-overdue financial transaction tax, which would help slow down out-of-control speculation as well as create enormous resources that could be put to good use. Regulators simply cannot keep up with the waves of 'financial innovation' and book-keeping evasions in this world of paper wealth that is, ironically, called 'securitization'. It is not clear whether the bankers themselves are really on top of this either.

Controlling finance is crucial to degrowth for many reasons. One is certainly that, as we have seen, growth rates have stagnated across the industrial world, affecting particularly the economic share occupied by wages. Unions and public regulation have been weakened by waves of neoliberal enthusiasm for private market solutions. People's real incomes have fallen, creating not only political discontent but also a fall-off in the consumer confidence and demand so badly needed by the growth machine. To offset this, economies have been flooded by credit at almost all levels. This has fueled both a kind of skin-deep paper prosperity and an underlying fragility derived from individuals with over-extended mortgages and maxed-out credit cards and from major financial institutions who find their debt exceeds their ability to sustain their cashflow. In the meantime the system is kept going not only by the addiction to cheap credit but also by the fabulous bonuses and personal wealth flowing to those on top of the financial-services industry. In short, there is every reason to underpin a program of egalitarian degrowth by democratizing the access to capital. Only by making finance a public service will we gain the chance to redesign it to serve society's goals of distributional fairness and ecological sanity.

There is a long and complicated debate amongst those who would redirect or at least apply regulatory controls to the global flows of private capital. This is beyond the scope of what we can cover here. But it is safe to say that there is a plethora of ideas and policies that might achieve this. What is missing is the political will to move beyond timid (and easily evaded) attempts at making finance capital follow a set of rules and instead to encourage the establishment of public stocks of capital. A good popular summary of the potential for democratic control of capital is an excellent piece in *Jacobin* magazine by Seth Ackerman entitled 'The Red and the Black'.[3] He draws on a vision of the control of capital developed by dissident economists in the last days of Eastern European communism. The desire of Polish economists Wlodzimierz Brus and Kazimierz Laski was to maintain public control of the economy while getting rid of the waste, shortages and misallocation of resources associated with state socialist central planning. Their vision was straightforward enough: 'a constellation of autonomous firms, financed by a multiplicity of autonomous banks or investment funds, all competing and interacting in a market – yet all nevertheless socially owned.'

For Ackerman, this provides a starting-point for developing creative tactics to take hold of capital flows and socialize capital markets. 'Start with the basics. Private control over society's productive infrastructure is ultimately a financial phenomenon. It is by financing the means of production that capitalists exercise control, as a class or as individuals. What's needed, then, is a socialization of finance — that is, a system of common, collective financing of the means of production and credit.'

He foresees the development of a common fund as a source of stable investment and goes on to spell out what this might mean in practice: 'The common fund can now re-establish a "tamed" capital market on a socialized basis, with a multiplicity of socialized banks and investment funds owning and allocating capital among the means of production.'

There are many examples of public credit-granting institutions that already play this role in a small way. They can provide a template for how running finance as a public service rather than as a profit-seeking enterprise might work. Take the publicly owned State Bank in the conservative midwest US state of North Dakota. The Bank was established under the influence of the populist movement that swept the region before World War One, in reaction to the manipulation of capital markets by private banks in the financial centers such as New York and Chicago. The North Dakota State Bank has now existed for 90 years and provides not only loans at reasonable rates but also uses criteria aside from quick profit in making decisions that benefit the community as a whole. State and local governments are able to use it to bank public monies and issue bonds for significantly less than the big private banks would charge. The Bank's profits go back into the public coffers. The State Bank's executives work for a fraction of the millions paid to their Wall Street equivalents. The Bank is not involved in tax evasion, does not act as a high-risk casino and is the sober recipient of all public tax funds raised by local government.[4]

There is a growing interest in the state bank model, with some

20 other US state legislatures looking into the possibility of creating their own public banks. The public banking movement is being spearheaded by the Public Banking Institute, created back in 2011 to advocate for an alternative to the powerful, globalized private banks. Of course, to make the use of capital truly democratic we will need a mix of government-linked, community and co-operative financial institutions. In the US there are now around 7,000 community banks scattered across the country. There is a vibrant sector of different forms of financial co-operatives and credit unions almost everywhere that could provide the basis of an alternative to the private banking industry. In some areas, such as the Canadian province of Quebec, the financial sector is actually dominated by co-operatives such as the multi-billion-dollar Caisse Desjardins, which is not only the largest financial institution in the province but also the biggest private employer. One problem is that the tone and thrust of the world of finance as set by speculative banking encourages an inbuilt tendency for the entire sector to mimic the practices of the global highrollers. But a shift in the regulations and policy framework towards a system of democratic degrowth could be based on these germs of co-operative capital.

Unfortunately, in a number of cases the movement is in exactly the opposite direction – the demutualization of British building societies and the individualizing of many other co-operative efforts is the tenor of the times. An important example is the push to privatize the huge deposits held in post office savings bank systems in dozens of countries. In Japan, this system is the repository of one of the biggest pools of capital in the world, and its potential privatization makes the world's mega-banks drool in anticipation. But fiscally conservative Japanese savers are less than enthusiastic. Privatization has been slow, which is fortunate because the postal capital was therefore available for the rebuilding of the country's tsunami-shattered infrastructure in 2011. Without it, the money would have had to come from foreign lenders on draconian financial and political terms. As one observer points out:

> 'The Japanese people are intensely patriotic, however, and they are not likely to submit quietly to domination by foreigners. They generally like their government because they feel it is serving their interests. Hopefully the Japanese government will have the foresight and the fortitude to hang onto its colossal publicly owned bank and use it to leverage its people's savings into the credit needed to rebuild its ravaged infrastructure, avoiding a crippling debt burden to foreign interests.'[5]

While the idea of publicly controlled capital is not new, it has fallen out of favor in an era when the big mega-banks trumpet their creativity in handling our money, which they seem to think borders on genius. Privatization and demutualization have provided some short-term relief for deficit-plagued governments and debt-ridden consumers looking for quick cash. But a program of commonly held capital with competing publicly held financial institutions will make a major contribution to ending the yawning inequality gap. It is hard to imagine a future of convivial and democratic degrowth without this fundamental shift.

The wage-labor system

The main way in which income is currently distributed under capitalism is through wage labor. This was identified by Marx and a number of other critics as the key element in extracting the surplus that made the system work. Yet most state socialist systems, although supposedly opposing capitalism's exploitation of the worker, have made little headway in doing away with wage labor. Instead they have simply replaced private capitalists with state institutions as the employers of wage labor and (in the case of Stalinist communism) restricted the rights of workers to organize and strike for better conditions. If they have changed the equation at all it is in the area of social provision outside the system of production. Wage labor as a sphere of 'unfreedom' directed by an external management continues intact under both social democracy and Soviet-style communism. Talk of workers' self-management and control has in most cases remained at the level of empty slogans. The abolition of wage labor is put off to some distant future stage of fully evolved communism.

Of course, the only thing worse than having a job is not having one. Because the income from a job is the only way for most people to have any income at all (outside the shrinking ranks of small farmers and artisans) jobs, especially 'good jobs', are the currency by which the performance of the system is judged. For most people, losing your job means your livelihood disappears. Everyone promises jobs. Corporations claim that if they are not given the freedom to pollute and exploit they will not be able to 'create' jobs or, worse, will have to destroy existing ones. Politicians claim that if their policies are not implemented it will cost jobs. Conventional economics holds that without allowing the free play of market forces employment levels will surely fall. Trade unions and the left wing of the growth coalition push for policies they think of as job-friendly – their answer to fighting austerity is to restart the growth machine.

Many critics of the system believe the best course is to 'humanize' jobs but are reluctant to challenge the centrality of the wage-labor system itself as the main way of distributing society's wealth. This centrality accounts for the glorification of work, no matter how ill-paid or mind-numbing the job, and no matter how socially retrograde or ecologically damaging is its impact. The armaments industry employs millions. Millions more are now employed in the security industry (rent-a-cops), one of the few 'professions' that still shows marked growth. Other big employers in the chemical, petrochemical, industrial agriculture and extractive industries also provide work – but at an ecological price that future generations will be paying for many decades to come. Still, it is hard to find anyone critical of the 'jobs consensus'.

> '*The glorification of work as a prototypically human endeavor, as the key both to one's humanity and one's individuality, constitutes the fundamental ideological foundation of contemporary capitalism – it was built on the basis of this work ethic and it continues to serve the system's interests and rationalize its outcomes... The valorization of unalienated labor is no longer, if it ever was, an adequate strategy by which to contest contemporary modes of capitalist command [–] it is too readily co-opted in a context in which the metaphysics of labor and the moralization of work carry so much cultural authority.*'[6]

The author of this passage, Kathi Weeks, is sympathetic to the autonomist tradition of the Left identified with Michael Hardt and Antonio Negri. This perspective, discussed in Chapter 9, is known for its 'refusal of work', which it sees as marking a kind of exit rather than simply an opposition to the rule of capital. But, while the autonomists should be congratulated for breaking with job worship, they give few hints as to what a society not organized around the wage-labor system would look like.

If we are to overcome our job addiction, with all its psychological discontents and ecological fallout, another framework for distributing society's wealth is essential. This is where the notion of a program for the democratic management of our commonwealth is fundamental. In the view of some critics this must involve a kind of individual basic wage to which all are constitutionally entitled, part of a thicket of collective social wages: free education, healthcare and legal representation; eco-friendly public transportation; and a convivial infrastructure of common spaces as well as recreational and cultural opportunities. The costs of sustaining this productive infrastructure should take first priority when social wealth is divided up, before any provision for private consumption sets in. The road to a significant social wage has been to some extent traveled by social democratic states in northern Europe, which have succeeded (encouraged by the persistent demands of their citizens) in establishing a framework of services addressing retirement, childcare, maternity and paternity leave, unemployment, special needs, extensive vacations and much more. These programs are never entirely adequate (and far too often governed by a means-testing bureaucracy) and are also under constant pressure of being rolled back by market enthusiasts and their corporate sponsors. Yet, where they exist, a popular expectation has taken hold that this is an essential way of distributing at least some of society's wealth.

This 'social wage' needs to be supplemented by an individualized wage (a basic minimum income payment) that, in combination with adequate collective services, could provide the means of basic economic survival for all. This kind of individualized payment is less well established in practice. Back in the halcyon days of high growth rates after World War Two, which carried through to the 1960s and 1970s, there was a lively public discussion about a Guaranteed Annual Income as a way of providing for all. In 1966 the prolific British futurist economist Robert Theobald made the case for it in his book *The Guaranteed Income*:

> 'If a man [sic] is inherently irresponsible and a bum, the Guaranteed Income is undoubtedly the most stupid idea that anybody has yet managed to come up with. If, on the other hand, you believe in the long run that human beings can become responsible, can rise to the responsibility of developing themselves in our society, then the Guaranteed Income is the only thing, in my opinion, which will begin to lead us into a free society.'[7]

Theobald puts his finger on a key issue. Capitalism thrives on the notion of the lazy, unworthy worker and the idea that the human character can (and should) be reduced to self-seeking individualism. Its proponents would have us reduce the rights and obligations of citizenship to that of the passive and usually resentful taxpayer. This mythical taxpayer is constantly engaged in a futile search to seek value for money. This is now buried very deep in our culture. The idea that all taxation is theft competes with the more sane and generous idea that it is the gift we give each other in order to have a caring society. But if there is to be any chance of overcoming this powerful nonsense, we need to be able to establish the notion that we are and should be our sister's and brother's keeper. If we don't win this battle, we are unlikely to win any others. And what better place is there to do this than in putting forward the notion that we all have the right to an adequate income?

Debate has swirled around how to fund a basic income, what would be an adequate level, how to administer the system, and over what effect it would have on taxes, investment and the labor market. Opposition has always been fierce, with dire warnings of everything from the dissolution of the human character to certain economic collapse. The neoliberal ascendancy from the 1980s onwards swept any idea of a guaranteed income off the table. Ironically, it is just now, in an era of rampant inequality in which there is no longer any secure notion of lifelong or even permanent employment (especially for the young just coming onto the labor market), that proposals for a guaranteed income should be having their greatest resonance. It is beyond our scope here to deal with the various models for providing a basic income for all except to say that this is a completely realizable goal, especially if the waste associated with inequality, frivolous mass consumption and militarism is shifted to investing in the common good. This need not be restricted to the 'wealthy world' but could be implemented everywhere, although levels and programs would inevitably vary according to context and cost of living. Brazil has already implemented an admittedly far from adequate *Bolsa Familia* that at least establishes the principle of a floor below which people will not be allowed to sink.

Loosening our ties to the job economy will also provide a

freedom benefit that could help reinvigorate and deepen our partial democracy. No longer will citizens be subjected to a habit-forming regime of obedience in their work lives but they will have more time and energy for political participation. The economic anxieties that plague the human character could be significantly reduced. No longer will capital be able to use the various forms of job blackmail to get its way on investment decisions. The case for an adequate universal social wage and guaranteed income seems particularly strong given the precarious nature of jobs in the neoliberal era and the current high rates of youth unemployment almost everywhere. Work will, of course, still be necessary but its scale can be reduced with an optimum of democratic self-management introduced into the workplace. It could then be supplemented by a range of individually and communally defined volunteer efforts to improve the quality of life and help repair the environmental damage done by unthinking economic growth.

'If labor becomes less productive in physical output, but 'more productive' in meaningfulness, conviviality and autonomy, the net effect of the change could be positive for well-being and energy savings, especially considering that production in absolute terms would decrease with degrowth.'[6]

Displacing the centrality of the wage system in distributing wealth will allow the emergence of smaller and slower forms of production that we already see valued in such initiatives as the slow food movement that Carlos Petrini and his colleagues have set in motion, initially in Italy but now spreading everywhere. This is the kind of trade-off (free time in place of consumer fantasy) that has at least the potential for rallying people to the banner of an alternative to the growth machine. Through example, education and agitation, here is a case to be made that our lives should and could be better than what is currently on offer from corporate capitalism. All around the Islamic world those who want something better and different have made their case by both figuratively and actually refusing to leave the public square. Certainly the results of their actions are mixed and slow but it is exactly this kind of stubborn bravery that we need if we as advocates of an alternative to capitalism are to be a presence that refuses to leave.

Exiting the maze

This book has tried to give a brief history of past alternatives to capitalism and some of the dead-end streets that have ended in failure, co-optation or worse. But it has also, I hope, teased out some of the threads of possibility from which a future alternative might be woven. These are various and the richness of their diversity will present a challenge for even the most skilled seamstress. There are those, such as indigenous radicalism, which draw from experiences predating capitalism and celebrate values that, in modified form, could help us live within the bounds of our ecological possibilities. There is a utopian tradition, often disparaged by the orthodox Left, which has the potential for helping us think imaginatively about the future. There is the radical reappraisal of the commons and how we need to expand its meaning and run it in a more democratic and sustainable way. There are political traditions of self-rule that keep re-asserting themselves (most recently in Latin America) from which we can draw hope that politics can be about more than the self-preservation of the prerogatives of the political class. Can such traditions learn to coexist creatively? The path, as they say, is made by walking.

It is hard to see change coming in an apocalyptic thunderclap. We must give up the notion that history will provide an end to itself with the emergence of some brilliant new dawn in which all problems will solve themselves. Seth Ackerman puts his finger on it – we need to be modest but ambitious at the same time.

'The notion that history will reach some final destination where social conflict will disappear and politics come to a close has been a misguided fantasy on the Left since its genesis. Scenarios for the future must never be thought of as final, or even irreversible; rather than regard them as blueprints for some future destination, it would be better to see them simply as maps sketching possible routes out of a maze. Once we exit the labyrinth, it's up to us to decide what to do next.'[3]

Those of us working towards an alternative need to be able to combine the practical with the visionary. Practical in the sense of workable proposals that enable people to imagine how their lives can and should be better; practical also in the sense of allowing people the paradoxical possibility of more freedom as well as more security. But visionary enough to imagine a world where we can value things differently – and value ourselves not as individual achievers but as interacting subjects in supportive, reciprocal relationships. We do much of this already in our families, in our communities, in civil society, in our friendships, and even with complete strangers, through relationships of giving and solidarity. And this evidence gives the lie to the pessimistic notion of a human nature based solely on self-seeking and greed. It is mostly in the economy that the generous and thoughtful side of our nature is forced to dissolve in an acid of competitive insecurity. So if we use our imagination (both practical and visionary) we can grasp the possibility of reshaping economic life so that capital serves us rather than the other way around.

We can use Ackerman's maze metaphor to build a practical notion of species survival that is in tune with the ecological possibilities. This will not be some bounteous utopia where all significant human problems disappear but rather a world that builds upon our better natures. I have sketched out here one potential way out of the maze that involves a democratic degrowth underpinned by the common control of capital and a universal basic income. There will be many other exit points, many other routes. But the need to find those ways out of the maze is urgent since, if the present momentum of the system is left unchecked, we will be heading over an economic and ecological cliff. We have decades, not centuries, to turn this around. There is no scientific certainty here. No inevitable communism embedded in the history of class struggle. But there is still just a chance (even if the odds are long) of saving our sad and beautiful world.

1 Karin de Miguel Wessendorf, Heinrich Böll Foundation, 31 Jan 2013, degrowthcanada.wordpress.com **2** Donald MacKenzie, 'How the Banks Do It', *London Review of Books*, 9 May 2013. **3** Seth Ackerman, 'The Red and the Black' , *Jacobin*, 1 Dec 2012, jacobinmag.com **4** Les Leopold, 'North Dakota, Socialist Haven?' *Salon*, 29 Mar 2013, salon.com **5** Ellen Brown, ' Japan Post's Stalled Sale A Saving Grace', *Asia Times*, 1 Apr 2011, atimes.com **6** Kathi Weeks, 'The Refusal of Work as Demand and Perpective', in *The Philosophy of Antonio Negri*, eds Murphy & Mustapha, Pluto, 2005. **7** Lynn Chancer, 'Benefiting from Pragmatic vision, Part One', in *Post-work*, eds Aronowitz & Cutler, Routledge, 1998.

Index